Flying
Bomb

Flying Bomb

Peter G. Cooksley

ROBERT HALE · LONDON

© *Peter G. Cooksley 1979*
First published in Great Britain 1979

ISBN 0 7091 7399 7

Robert Hale Limited
Clerkenwell House
Clerkenwell Green
London, EC1

Photoset by
Specialised Offset Services Limited, Liverpool
and printed in Great Britain by
Lowe & Brydone Limited,
Thetford, Norfolk

Contents

Illustrations

Line Drawings in Text

Picture Credits

The author is indebted to the following archives and persons for permission to reproduce the photographs used to illustrate this book:

Argus Newspapers Limited of Redhill, Surrey, the present owners of the photographs originally taken for the former *Croydon Times* series of newspapers

Norman W. Cruwys

The Imperial War Museum, Lambeth

The Royal Aircraft Establishment, Farnborough, Hants

The Royal Observer Corps

Other photographs are from the author's collection

The cartoon originally appeared in the issue of the *Aeroplane* for 24 November 1944 and is reproduced by permission of *Aeroplane Monthly* and the artist, R. Brockbank

Maurice Allward's sketch in Chapter Four and his map in Chapter Five are reproduced with his permission and that of *Aviation News* in the columns of which they first appeared.

Acknowledgement

The author gratefully acknowledges his indebtedness to the following persons who have so readily drawn on their memories or assisted in various measure and a variety of ways in supplying material for this work.

Maurice Allward
Miss Constance Babington Smith, OBE
Mrs D.J. Baker
Howard E. Bentley
Miss June Broughton
Wing Commander Roland P. Beaumont, CBE, DSO+, DFC+, FRAeS
Douglas J.S. Cluett, ALA
Norman W. Cruwys
Mr and Mrs B.W. Draper
The Rt. Hon. Lord Duncan Sandys, PC, CH, MA
Mrs Crystal H.N. Finch
Michael A. Fopp
A.K. Henderson, BEM
P.S. Laurie, MBE
D. Bruce Robertson
John W.R. Taylor, FRHistS, MRAeS, FSLAET

Preface

This is not a technical book and what technicalities there are
have been banished to a series of appendices at the back so
that the result is confidently believed to be a "plain tale,
simply told".

The attacks by flying bombs and the even more hideously
alarming V-2 rockets came at a time when a vast number of
occurrences were taking place in all corners of the world, with
the result that they have tended to be overshadowed by events
and largely ignored by historians so that this is an attempt to
remedy the situation for, if only for the fact that 'doodle bugs'
were the harbingers of a new type of warfare, their history is
worth recording in some depth.

Our memories all tend to sift the exciting or even the
amusing and pleasant from the horrible or distressing and
retain only the former as time passes, with the result that there
is, at present, an enormous interest in the war years. This is
not only confined to those who have recollections of the events
but is also strong among those who missed them by virtue of
being elsewhere and among the young people to whom the
Second World War is something which the earlier generation
talk about. With this in mind an attempt has been made to
provide as near as possible something of a 'handbook' on the
subject so that armchair tacticians, specialist historians and
even model builders, those painstaking people who have done
so much for military history, will find something of value in
these pages, which contain much which is new on the subject.

London, 1978   PETER G. COOKSLEY

1 | No New Thing

"The thing that hath been, it is that which shall be; and that which is done is that which shall be done: and there is no new thing under the sun."

Ecclesiastes 1:9

The Finch family, mother, daughter and teenage son had been out of their beds since late the previous night. They had spent an uncomfortable few hours sitting on the bedless bunk frames in their 'Anderson' air-raid shelter at the bottom of the garden to which they had retreated in something like surprise after the siren had woken them. Surprise, because there had been no 'alerts' for a very long time and the war was almost over. It simply could not last much longer now; the steady tones of General Eisenhower had announced the invasion of the continent of Europe on 6 June, only ten days before, and the newspapers daily assured readers that things were going well and that 1944 was to see the liberation of Nazi-held territories everywhere.

Their time in the shelter had been all the more difficult to endure because absolutely nothing had happened in their quiet, select part of suburbia, fourteen miles south of London. "The chap who sounds the 'all clear' must have nodded off," they had joked and had straight away gone back to the house.

Once indoors they stood about disconsolately, hands thrust deep into the pockets of dressing-gowns thrown over night clothes, and waited. Scarcely audible in the distance a clock struck four and then the silence descended again, perhaps not so complete as it had been, for a long way off something was buzzing, a motor cycle perhaps? Yes, it was closer now and had an odd note about it that did not seem to come from the road but rather above. Soon the sound filled everything and it was obviously no motor cycle but an aeroplane with a rough note to its engine. The family tensed, the noise was overhead and had reached a crescendo. An aeroplane, with engine trouble and about to crash! "Down!" said the daughter firmly and the three dropped onto the carpet. At the same moment there was an explosion like a roll of thunder and the boy was in time to see the French doors, uncurtained against the summer night but fastened and bolted, flung open, not violently but seemingly almost slowly, as if cast back by a leisurely, giant hand. At the same moment the fixed windows swung out as if hinged and remained hanging precariously.

Mentally dazed for only a moment by the sudden eruption of the violence, the Finch family were quickly on their feet. The first to speak was the son, "That was a bomber shot down with its load on board!" he stated with the confidence of youth, "I'm going to have a look!" For a moment his mother protested in the doorway and then, caught up in the excitement of the moment, both she and her daughter decided to join him.

By the sounds of activity, the incident was evidently quite near and the eager youth strode a little ahead of the others up the blacked-out street. Quite suddenly his foot caught something which went spinning with a metallic tinkle; he stooped and picked it up. "What's that you've got?" enquired a female air-raid warden as she crossed the road, "This," he replied, holding out a jagged, triangular piece of metal. "Feel, it's still hot."

Round the corner some 200 yards away was a scene of chaos; scattered about the pavement was a great quantity of wood, broken and splintered, while four semi-detached houses appeared to have had their fronts punched by a gigantic fist so that the middle pair were reduced to nothing more than the rear walls. Roofs in the vicinity which had remained in position had been flung into an angry sea of tiles. Across the debris which had been their home a mother and daughter picked a careful path, the girl with a black, glossy raincoat over her pyjamas looking very different from the statuesque, leggy, barefooted blonde in a dancer's brief costume who gazed out from the prints displayed in a near-by photographer's window.

Across the road a great waste of masonry and wreckage marked the site of the detached house which had received the main force of the explosion while, in the middle of the road, a fireman, with seeming unconcern, played a light hose on a small fire at his feet, the flames illuminating in an unreal glow the milling throng of wardens, rescue workers, police and firemen.

Above the sounds of their endeavour rose another strange engine beat. "Watch out!" cried one of the men, "he's still about up there!"

A quarter of a mile away the family of young Finch's girlfriend was better informed. Father, mother, son and daughter had all climbed onto the top of their air-raid shelter to gain a better view and were listening to their eldest, a Sergeant Pilot on leave, who was destined to die with his crew in a Lancaster bomber over Harburg only five months later.

This, he told them, was a new and different weapon, a small aeroplane which, without a crew or any human guidance, flew with explosive to its target and destroyed itself there; in fact, a flying bomb.

There was nothing new in the idea of a weapon of this sort and there is reason to believe that pioneering work, at least in the field of unmanned flight, can be traced back as far as 1891 to the ingenious Sir Hiram Maxim. But the application of this principle to an offensive vehicle seems to have been first attempted by Professor A.M. Low who, in the First World War, was asked to develop a radio-controlled aeroplane by the War Office which intended it to be used for attacks against heavily defended ground targets and to intercept Zeppelins. At the time he was already working at the Woolwich Ordnance College to develop a new range-finder for coastal artillery but, approached on the new project, he was commissioned as a Second Lieutenant and, with a small staff, moved to a garage at Chiswick.

Here, he was approached by the security-minded Director of Military Aeronautics with the words, "Now, Low, we must think of some thundering lie to conceal the fact that we have a new weapon; let us call it the A.T., people will think it is meant as an aerial target."

In fact Low was only responsible for work on radio guidance systems for the missile and it turned out to be bulky and cumbersome, as was to be expected from the heavy components of the day. While this was going on, a veil of complete secrecy was maintained over the RFC Experimental Works, as the unit became known, and went to such extremes as the posting of police guards at a new works at Brooklands and orders never being published in the gazette.

The aeroplane into which the radio equipment was eventually fitted was a shoulder-wing monoplane with a cylindrical fuselage, skid gear underneath and an uncowled 50 hp Gnome rotary motor. Indeed, it was this engine which was the undoing of the missile since, under test, it caused so much interference with the radio that it rapidly became obvious that flying it was impracticable. The date was October 1916.

Although these tests at Upavon had to be abandoned, it was by no means the end of the project, since several other manufacturers were designing air-frames to use the radio equipment, a feature common to nearly all being the intention that they be launched with the aid of a trolley. This was true of the neat little monoplane with a 22-foot wing span which was produced next, by a team from the Royal Aircraft Factory at Farnborough which included the young Geoffrey de Havilland working under the guidance of H.P. Folland. The motor was of the horizontally-opposed twin-cylinder type delivering 35 hp; it was the work of Granville Bradshaw of ABC, employing low-grade materials and intended for a life of as little as two hours. It appears that this was the A.T. which was presented to a gathering of senior officers at Upavon on 21 March 1917 where Low with his assistants, who included Captain Poole and Lieutenants Bowen and Whitton, were anxious to demonstrate that the idea General Caddell of the War Office had envisaged about two years previously was a practical one. Unfortunately, the day was not crowned with success and the little aeroplane rushed across the aerodrome, gained a negligible altitude and then crashed on the grass a few yards' away. In the silence which followed one of the invited spectators, Major Gordon Bell, as famed for his stammer as much as for his trenchant remarks, could be heard saying, "I could throw my b-b-b-b-bloody umbrella further than that!"

In common with most of the designs of the period and, indeed, with the Nazi flying bomb of twenty-seven years later, this weapon lacked ailerons for lateral control. Perhaps this was intended to be achieved by wing warping but the Farnborough design certainly had a sharp dihedral angle to the wings so that it seems likely that this was intended to preserve stability.

Another attempt to produce a flying bomb was made at Kingston-upon-Thames by the Sopwith Company which built a biplane with a box-like fuselage into which was fitted another 35 hp ABC motor. To ensure a straight take-off a four-wheeled undercarriage was fitted and the aerials were wrapped round the upper wings outboard of the interplane struts and the rear fuselage. Taken to Feltham, it was in course of erection by a joint team of Royal Aircraft Factory and Sopwith Company staff and it is believed it was then that it was damaged so that further tests on this design were abandoned.

While this work was proceeding in Great Britain, similar considerations were being examined abroad. The most successful of these design studies was that for the American Curtiss-built Hewitt-Sperry biplane; radio controlled, it first flew on 12 September 1916 fitted with a 40 hp motor enabling it to carry for a distance of about 50 miles (80 kilometres) a

17

war-head containing 300 pounds (140 kilogrammes) of explosive. But perhaps the nearest in concept to the Nazi V-1 flying bomb was the Kettering Aerial Torpedo of 1918, this had an all-up weight of 530 pounds (240 kilogrammes), including 180 pounds (81 kilogrammes) of explosive, and had a range only a little less than the Curtiss.

However, work continued in this country after the Armistice of 1918 and two years later a standard Bristol F.2B was fitted with radio control and flew with success at Farnborough with a check pilot aboard in case it ran amuck. The lessons learnt from these experiments were put to use in a seriously-designed flying bomb, the Larynx of 1927, which, with a 250-pound (113 kilogramme) war-head, proved itself capable of flying accurately along a planned course off Devon, Cornwall and Somerset. Five of these were built and sent to Iraq for operational trials with Number 84 Squadron RAF at their base at Shaibah; of these, one was lost on launching, three came to premature ends due to troubles with the engines and fuel systems, while the final one vanished without trace.

There was certainly nothing new therefore, in the idea of a flying bomb but none of them was ever used in operational service (even the Kettering machine from America, the first missile to rejoice in the sobriquet of 'bug') so that the claim to fame of all this collection is in the field of comedy. It is part of the folk-lore of aviation that one of the A.T.s from Farnborough in the early days (there seem to have been six assembled) of the same type which had brought forth the comment from Gordon Bell, was being demonstrated on another occasion, when it suffered from loss of signal and immediately went into a near-vertical dive above the assembled dignitaries, many of them clad in the magnificent full-dress uniforms of the age. It is recorded that watchers saw the group hesitate for a moment before scattering to every point of the compass with remarkable speed, rather like witnessing the sudden opening of some gaudy tropical bloom!

Having considered the historical aspects of the concept of a flying bomb, which was taken up as much in Germany as elsewhere well before the advent of the Nazis, with the Schmidt proposals, based on studies carried out in 1928 and more fully described in the next chapter, it is time to look into the state of preparedness for an assault by an entirely new type of weapon and the heralding of a completely new concept in warfare.

The British people had been conditioned to the idea of bombardment from the air long before the outbreak of war in 1939. To some extent, the beginnings of this had been laid as long before as 1915 by such attacks as that which provoked the *Daily News and Leader* on Tuesday 1 June to fling across its front page the headline "Zeppelin Raid Over Outer London", continuing "Many Fires Reported but These not Absolutely Connected with Airships". Furthermore the audacious flight in an LVG biplane by Deck Offizier Paul Brandt with his observer Leutnant Walther Ilges, which enabled them to place six bombs near Victoria Station on 28 November of the following year and thus to pave the way for the great Gotha daylight raids during 1918, had also caused the population to realize that Great Britain was no longer an island. The generation then unborn received their early ideas on this subject from the popular magazines between the wars which attempted to widen their circulation by peddling fear, with sentimental cover pictures of children at bed-time prayer wearing gas masks. Even seemingly responsible writers who were in a position to ascertain the truth, flung aside their training as journalists and vied with each other in attempts to make their readers' flesh creep.

After the war began, the spreading of "alarm and despondency" was made an offence, and this effectively silenced these writers. The RAF's victory in the Battle of Britain and the constant praise for civilians had boosted morale and this had been sustained by such items in the Press as the May 'bag' of night raiders being claimed as 156 towards the end of the blitz of 1941; while the reports of the sporadic daylight visitations by the *Luftwaffe* during 1942 and 1943 were to be found among such items as the increase of the sweet

19

ration to 4 ounces each per week, and that the king had received birthday congratulations by telegram from the Soviet President, Mr Kalinin.

By the beginning of the following year, a note of optimism had crept in and crooners on the radio were looking forward to the day "When they sound the last All Clear"; the sirens were still in position and maintained in working order but were now largely silent. But about the civil defence workers, the successors to the old ARP, who had distinguished themselves so well during the night bombing, doubts were being freely expressed; they had become 'soft' people said and spent much of their time playing cards, setting up gambling dens where the "low way of passing the time must be abolished ... at least on Sunday".

To the ordinary civilian, by the time that 1944 was being written on the date-line, the private air-raid shelter at the bottom of his garden had become accepted, hardly thought about and little used. If it was an 'Anderson' underground type as likely as not it was landscaped for the cultivation of vegetables where it protruded above the soil, maybe scratched over by hens, which even office workers were now keeping at the end of the little patches which did duty as gardens behind their suburban 'three-up and two-downs'. Probably, too, the 'Anderson' was flooded with rain water. These shelters were simply built from corrugated sections, each two feet four inches wide and arched so that they could be bolted together at the top. Each risement was about five inches broad so that, with overlaps, families of two adults issued with four sections sheltered in a structure only about four feet long; larger families rating six sections had a shelter with an assembled length of six feet, which permitted the erection of bunks so that whole nights could be spent under cover. The back and front were each closed with three more flat corrugated panels, the middle one at the front being divided to provide a doorway at ground level. One had to step onto a box or stool inside before jumping down to the floor so it was impossible to walk straight into an 'Anderson', even if you were lucky enough to have the type of soil which permitted sufficiently deep excavation for the whole thing to go under the earth. In the open aperture many people put light doors and it was customary to have a 'blast wall', a hollow structure of brick filled with earth, or perhaps just a stout pile of sand-bags to protect the opening against the entry of splinters.

A rectangle of light 'L'-section girders provided a frame at the base and another lent strength half-way up, and level with this at the back was a panel, similar in size to the entrance, which was retained in position by a pair of heavy brackets, each like an inverted capital 'L', bolted to the central frame. This was an escape hatch and a heavy spanner was also supplied to unfasten these before removing the metal sheet and tackling the earth covering with the spade that most people kept handy in case soil flung from a crater or a building collapse should block the entry and oblige them to make their exit through the rear.

By the time of the Nazi final throw against Great Britain, many families, who had evacuated themselves, or sent their children to the country under the government scheme, had returned only to find that the 'Anderson' which they had refused before the war, was now no longer to be had. Some sporadic air raids were still going on and the chances of obtaining an underground refuge were nil, due to the metal shortage, which had by this time accounted for the disappearance of ornamental chains dividing their front gardens and the railings, not only domestic but those about parks and cemeteries as well. Nevertheless, despite a paper shortage, a receipt was always carefully issued to householders!

To meet this new demand, new shelters of brick construction and wholly on the surface were hastily erected. These also were of two types, for small and larger families, and looked for all the world like small, stout garden sheds with thick concrete roofs, pitched like that of a house and with entrances permitting entry with only a slight stoop by all except the tallest. Indeed, even now, there are many of these still to be seen in the older sections of our towns, but for the most part, survivors of these quaint erections have had windows cut through the walls whereas they were quite dark inside during the days of their original use.

Ordinary civilians had now accepted all these things as part of their way of life along with the coal, stacked five feet high in the London parks and stretching as far as the eye could see; the "Announcements" programme on the radio, along with Sandy Macpherson at the organ; messages from British children in Australia; "Works Wonders"; the Albert Sandler Trio and "Those Were the Days". At the cinema you could admire Betty Grable's legs, Deanna Durbin's voice or follow the war news, which never escaped you, from British Movietone, "presenting the truth to the free peoples of the world". Afterwards, as he made up his Unity Pool coupon (cut from the newspaper) combining Littlewoods, Vernons, Copes and Shermans with such now forgotten Pools as Socapools, Bonds, Jervis and Screen, many a man pondered the words of Leslie Mitchell in the newsreel commentary, – that "British bombers had pounded enemy targets in France with 23,000 tons of high explosive!" – causing him to wonder whatever could be there to call for all that number of bombs, and in France too, so close to us? He would have been surprised could he have known that the bombers were intent on the destruction of bases for a weapon which Great Britain could have then held in large numbers, for the equivalent had existed in concept since 1940 in the form of the Miles 'Hoopla', but the project had been throttled, at the first suggestion, by alarmed officialdom.

2 | 'Cherrystone'

During the years between the two World Wars, several nations carried out experiments into the possibilities of various forms of unmanned bomber. These were to be directed to their target either by radio or automatic pilot. In view of this, the suggestion placed before the Nazi German Air Ministry, the Reichsluftfahrtministerium (RLM) in 1939, not long after the outbreak of hostilities, was not as impractical as it may at first seem. That the proposal was rejected was no reflection on the potential use of such a weapon, but rather that, since the distances from which it had to be launched were moderately long, there could be no means whereby military and civilian areas would be distinguished. It must also be realized that this decision was taken in the light of events in Poland where the amazing advances of the Panzer Divisions with air support from the *Luftwaffe*'s 'Stukas' indicated a short, sharp conflict which would possibly culminate with a peace settlement with Great Britain, allowing a concentration of Hitler's military might, against which seemingly nothing could stand, in other directions. Over and above all this was the fact that such a missile's motor would perforce be of the conventional piston type such as was fitted to all the earlier models in attempts to perfect such a weapon over the short preceding period of about twenty years, so that cost considerations had also to be taken into account.

As events turned out, it was inter-service rivalry as much as strategic requirements that gave birth to the world's first operational missile, although even then it would not have been possible had it not been for the existence of the reaction-propulsion motor.

Early in 1942 it was common knowledge in Nazi military circles that the Army was contemplating the bombardment of targets in England by means of explosive-carrying rockets which were being developed with some prospect of success near the Baltic village of Peenemünde. This caused concern in *Luftwaffe* circles that the private venture of the *Wehrmacht* would soon be rivalling their traditional role as the hammer of London which was, at that particular moment, making heavy demands on their resources which had to be stretched, not only to carry out some measure of reprisal for the mounting intensity of RAF attacks on German targets, but also to fly on the Russian Front, together with operations of lesser strength elsewhere.

It therefore seemed the ideal solution when, in March of the same year Fieseler Werke's Robert Lusser mentioned his interest in the well-aired theories of a flying bomb to the co-ordinating engineer of the RLM. In the event, the observation seemed providential for, three years earlier, the same authority had directed Argus Motorenwerke to explore the possibilities of a small, cheap pulse-jet and the development team under the leadership of Dr Fritz Gosslau had laid down the basic principles well before the withdrawal of Allied troops from Dunkirk, in fact in March 1940.

Not until then were they allowed access to another line of experiment which had been pursued by Paul Schmidt, the fluid dynamicist, since 1934 when his team had been snubbed by the RLM when its proposal for a flying bomb had been rejected as of doubtful use. The following year, this same authority had second thoughts following representations from the youthful von Braun, later of V-2 and inter-planetary rocket fame, and other scientists and engineers. Schmidt found his group suddenly in receipt of a generous grant from public funds to be directed towards the further development of the pulse-jet motor specified in connection with the flying bomb proposal. The resultant propulsion unit was known as the Schmidtrohr, and it was this which the Gosslau team was eventually allowed to examine, although they borrowed little from it except the valve system and a truncated form of the name; Schmidt's work, which was envisaged for purposes of assisted aircraft take-off never received its true recognition due to the inadequate funds subsequently awarded for its development.

The Argus pulse-jet showed itself capable of delivering about half the thrust of the earliest Schmidt motors when one flew for the first time at the end of April 1941, suspended beneath the Gotha 145, a two-seat training biplane resembling the British Tiger Moth.

There followed the most important single step in the development of the weapon, which was later to be known as the V-1, when, on 10 June 1942 an RLM scientific committee met under the chairmanship of Field Marshal Erhard Milch. At this meeting, he was shown by Dr Gosslau a rough sketch of the proposed design for a flying bomb, which might be powered by one of the new-type motors, and the Field Marshal's enthusiasm was seen to increase as the doctor, in reply to the questions put to him, launched into a description of the anticipated potential of the design. The culmination of this was that nine days later, the RLM decided to take a supreme gamble and an order of the highest priority was placed for the development and production of the flying bomb.

The work was to be undertaken jointly by the two interested firms and, while Fieseler would be responsible for the air-frame, others involved were Walters, who were to design the take-off ramp and its associated catapult and Siemens who were to develop the guidance system from the Askania autopilot. Since the overall responsibility for co-ordination and development was that of Fieseler Werke at Kassel, the designation Fieseler Fi 103 was adopted. However, in order to confuse Allied Intelligence, the device would also be known as the *Flak Ziel Gerät*, that is an anti-aircraft target apparatus, thus working along the same line of deception as the old A.T. ruse. The initials of the former description quickly came into common usage, so it is unfortunate that FZG could also be taken to mean *Fern Ziel Gerät* – long-range target apparatus. Thus the cover which this description provided for the project was limited to say the least!

Peenemünde was once more the venue for the first launches of the air-frame, not from the ground, but from underneath the four-engined Focke-Wulf FW 200 at the beginning of December 1942. A few weeks later, on Christmas Eve, the first launching of a powered missile was carried out.

The motor design had already been the subject of practical tests above carrier machines of the Junkers Ju 88 and Dornier Do 17 types, which suffered considerable damage during the work from the exhaust of the little pulse-jet, so that it was decided to mount them on the actual flying bombs with the rear of the pipe well clear of the controls.

Test-vehicle air-frames used for the first fitting of these motors may well have been the 'P 35' type which were no more than cylinders welded up from pressed mild steel with an aluminium alloy nose-cone and a ply wing.

Further tests during 1943 were disappointing, the December firing had achieved a range of only some 1,000 metres (1,100 yards) and frequent crashes occurred. At first this was thought to be due to vibration brought about by the crude principles on which the motor functioned and attention was given to the engine mounting, so arranged that it consisted of a single point at the top of the fin and a flexible fork at the leading edge, for, since it was recognized that the guidance and aiming of the weapons would be dependent on the compass, anything which would upset the accuracy of this would have to be minimized. No sooner had this malady been traced to errors in the design of the guidance servos which threw the missile out of control when subjected to a cross-wind, than a new series of crashes took place. Once again, the guidance system was suspect, and a series of launchings were carried out, according to Nazi propaganda of those years, with the diminutive girl Flugkapitän, Hanna Reitsch, borne aloft in an observation capsule built into the robot to determine, by means of a periscope, the reason for the wings to be shed when the change from climbing to level flight took place. After four days of this hazardous work, it was found that the torsion applied by the initial acceleration of the launcher was altering the angle of the wings which then broke away when normal flight was begun. This was corrected and the test programme went ahead with greater ease since, now that some measure of sustained flight could be expected, it was possible to collect data on seventeen variables transmitted by a form of telemetry, known as FuG 23, to an observation aircraft flying with the robot. In this way, it became possible to discover faults in the fuel system and the air intake to the pulse jet and correct them immediately, so that by May 1943 the project could be pronounced as "very hopeful".

One month later, positive steps were taken to begin using the flying bomb as an offensive weapon with the establishment at Zempin of the headquarters of the Lehr und Erprobungskommando Wachtel, named after its commander, Max Wachtel, to carry on the operational development, still over the sea, from the Baltic test establishment; while, only six weeks later saw the establishment of the Flak Regiment (so-called) which was to be responsible for the actual launching in France, the composition seemingly consisting of forty-eight platoons (*Züge*) in thirteen batteries, involving a total of about four thousand men. Site defence, communications and supply fell to the sections of the *Luftwaffe* which normally dealt with this sort of thing and was not the immediate concern of the Wachtel command.

The missiles which were employed were not the final perfected models but development specimens, so that the working out of launching procedures made slow progress, which was further frustrated during the following month when Operation 'Hydra' by the RAF, the massive attack on Peenemünde, described in detail in a later chapter, forced a move to Brüsterort in what is now East Germany. Here, the experiments went ahead with greater speed since the urgency of the situation for the Nazis was now becoming only too obvious and also bombs of the final, operational model were now available for the first time. It was about now that the codeword '*Kirschkern*' (Cherrystone) came into more common use for the new weapons. That these were a tremendous advance over the early machines in performance alone, was now plain to see, since the speed matched that of the best fighters of the day and was even superior to some and was such that, after the attacks began, the wooden noses of some intercepting British Mosquito fighters split during a fast tailchase.

Meanwhile, preparations were under way in the Cherbourg area of France for the erection of a series of concrete bunkers and ramps for the discharge of large numbers to the main target, London, although, with its range of 163 miles (260 kilometres), later extended to 250 miles (400 kilometres) by the carriage of extra fuel at the cost of a reduced war-head and with lighter, wooden, wings fitted, it was capable of going rather further afield.

Originally, it was anticipated that the first assault would take place around Christmas of that year, but the season came and went and no attack was begun. This was in part due to the very large number of modifications which were being incorporated on the production line, but it is probable that control of all 'secret weapons' being taken over by the 65th Army Corps on 1 December also had something to do with the delay.

Three months before this, the progress of events in enemy territory, carefully hidden as they were, convinced Dr R.V. Jones of Scientific Intelligence in London that, from the list he had been instructed to prepare at the outbreak of war, of possible new weapons likely to be flung at Britain and which included rockets, gas, death rays, biological warfare, magnetic mines and flying bombs, the last was next to be used. Consequently, a further delay for the Nazis was brought about by Allied attacks on those parts of the Continent likely to be the source of the bombs and simpler sites had to be begun protected by hastily erected log and earth barriers. This was

28

not immediately realized by British military authorities and some effort was wasted on sites which had been abandoned.

As befitted an expendable weapon, the FZG 76 was basically simple in concept, the majority of the external casing being welded up from 16-gauge mild steel sheet, although the covering for the tail unit and controls was somewhat lighter and was riveted to pressed steel ribs of about 22 gauge. Examination of several specimens showed that the workmanship was rough, with often crude assembly and poorly welded joins.

The nose which formed the first of six sections of the fuselage, was formed of an aluminium alloy cone of streamlined shape. At the front of this was a small 'windmill' or propeller by means of which the length of the flight was governed. The air from the forward thrust of the bomb caused this to rotate and the number of rotations was noted by a counter inside which had been set before launching for a predetermined number which would, when exhausted, cause the robot to re-set the controls from the flying position and to dive onto its target.

Immediately behind this mechanism, inside, was a hollow wooden sphere or ball containing the compass, which would guide the flight path. The purpose of the enclosure in wood was in order to provide a casing with some measure of shock proofing, which would also be non-magnetic and thus, avoid deflecting the compass bearing. Further protection against vibration was given by mounting the timber in a series of rubber suspension pads. However, these forms of protection for the master compass would not have been sufficient to ensure accuracy in an entirely steel construction. This would have exerted a considerable magnetic effect so it was dealt with by the process of 'compass swinging' for which special bases, away from the effect of magnetic interference, were set out at the launching sites. To term what went on as either a process or even as 'compass swinging' is to give a wholly erroneous impression, for the operation involved nothing more than pointing the missile in the direction of its target and then beating it with wooden mallets! The result of this vigorous arm exercise by *Luftwaffe* launching crews was to align the magnetic field of the mass of steel with the earth's field so that the pull exerted on the compass needle would not cause a deviation away from the course setting.

Separated from the nose section by a bulkhead of 14-gauge steel, lay the war-head of 'Amatol' high-blast effect explosive with, running through its core, the tubular, main fuse pocket. Set at an angle of some forty-five degrees to the horizontal from the fore part of this was a pair of fuse primers and the whole was connected to a pair of impact switches, one in the nose and a second, to be triggered by a belly landing, underneath. Reports at the time also suggest that at least some of the bombs were fitted with a time fuse as well.

This war-head had no internal shell, such as was later introduced on a modified version, and was bolted to the next section by means of four pairs of lugs and aligned by a narrow flange ring.

The mid point of the missile was formed by the fuel tank, the 'B-Stoff' (petrol), which accounted for 1,133 pounds (515 kilogrammes) of the weight. The two bulkheads forming the ends of this tank, were domes into the adjacent sections. Through the middle of this portion, passed a large horizontal hole with its tubular walls braced by a heavy web above to the lifting lug for reception of a chain from an overhead gantry by means of which the assembled missile was hoisted onto the end of the launching ramp. The tank filler cap lay forward of this lug. The tube for the main spar of the wings formed a sleeve through which it ran and was further braced downwards by another web which connected to the 'C' section launching rail, with a blind forward end for the lug from the launching ramp piston, welded on the outside of the case forming the wall of the fuel tank.

Immediately behind all this was another large section containing a pair of spherical compressed air bottles which, although staggered diagonally across their cradle, and strapped into fitting holes, rather after the fashion in which some Easter eggs are packed in presentation boxes, tended to fill, almost completely, the available space. In order to reinforce them against the internal pressure of some 900 pounds per square inch, these spheres were bound with wide bands of perforated 'wire' round the cast iron globes. Air lines from these bottles led to the next section, bolted on like the war-head with four pairs of external lugs, containing the 'Steurgerät'. This was a combined piece of equipment containing the master and secondary gyros which controlled the course of the bomb in the manner to be explained later, while also in this compartment was the fuel control mechanism, set above the petrol filter and the multiple dry battery for the electrical services. Situated low down on the port side of the forward part of this section was the inset starting connection point, while above, also on the same side, was a large removable access hatch via which the barometric altitude control, an aneroid capsule more familiar as a means of forecasting the weather in many a domestic hall, could be set.

The final fuselage section consisted of nothing more than a cone of steel sheet in which were mounted, on a horizontal base between the inner roots of the tailplane, the pneumatic servo-motors powered by the compressed air from the twin iron spheres. The air at this point had been reduced by means of a valve to a pressure of about 90 pounds psi, and was further reduced, when fed into these servos, to under 20 pounds pressure. These motors were the means by which the elevators and rudder, the latter activated by a horn and rod externally on the starboard side, were moved in the same way as used by a human pilot to guide an aeroplane. These control surfaces had a light metal skin as already mentioned. There were no ailerons.

The first wings of a flying bomb consisted of a set of pressed steel ribs of 'Z' section, that is to say they each had a short flange pointing in opposite directions above and below the main flat, making in fact a 'Z' with an upright, rather than a diagonal bar. These were fourteen in number per wing, and

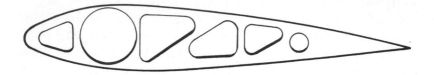

V-1 Metal Wing Rib

had five holes fretted out, the rear-most being circular, the others triangular, for lightness. At the point of maximum depth, one aperture back, was a circular hole measuring 11.5 centimetres ($4\frac{1}{2}$ inches) in diameter which took the tubular main spar right through the large sleeve in the fuel tank, already described. This spar fell short each side, by only three rib spaces, of the pressed steel wing-tips. The only other bracing was afforded by a flanged sheet metal rear spar and the sheet-steel skin which was riveted onto the rib flanges. At first the wings were not fitted with any form of cable cutter, but it became obvious that the barrier of balloons was constituting a serious obstacle, so these cutters, when they appeared, took one of two forms. The first was nothing more than a narrow strip of sharpened steel running the entire length of each wing leading edge, as shown in the drawing in Appendix 7. The other was slightly more refined and was inset into the outboard leading edge of the wing for a distance equal to five rib spacings.

The operating cycle for the Argus As 109-014 Rohr motor began with the fuel, of which 640 litres (140 gallons) were carried in the original type of tank, being forced by compressed air into the forward, widest part of the propulsion unit through a set of three banks of atomizers, with three nozzles in each. Here it was mixed with air and detonated at the start of a launch by a single Bosch sparking plug in the top of the chamber. The air was provided by the forward thrust of the missile and entered the same chamber via multiple rows of valves, a little like spring clothes-pegs but of metal. It was in these arrays of valves that the banks of atomizers were set. The resultant explosion inside the combustion chamber had the effect of forcing these valves momentarily closed, while, at the same time, the resultant gas was partially compressed by a set of venturis, like shelves with oval cross-sections. The only way out for the pressure was backwards, through the tapering portion of the jet unit, so that it was further compressed and issued from the rear pipe with such force that it exerted thrust and the reaction propelled the missile forward. The cycle then resumed but after launching the residual flame on the inside walls of the unit was sufficient to ignite the further mixtures of petrol and air so that the sparking plug was no longer required. The complete chain of operation took place at a rate of 42 per second and in so doing produced the characteristic 'two-stroke' sound which excited such comment when first heard over England.

The launching sites which were used when Operation '*Rumpelkammer*' was finally begun, six months late as it turned out, bore little resemblance to the elaborate structures originally planned. The fact that there were any at all was entirely due to Section E8 of the Karlshagen Establishment which devised a much simpler ramp and associated services that could be fairly swiftly erected in densely-wooded parts of the Pas de Calais, where they would be extremely difficult to see from the air. These were reasonably simple and could be assembled in such a way that they would blend with farm buildings and small clusters of dwellings.

The main piece of equipment was the essential Walter catapult which consisted of a long, inclined track some 48 metres (150 feet) in length supported on log uprights with some additional steel girders hidden under the shadow of the massive rail; the whole carefully braced and trussed so that it provided a firm launching platform. For the whole length of this ramp, which was assembled in sections, ran a tube, open at the top by virtue of a narrow slot in the upper surface of the rail. Into this firing tube was fitted a type of piston having the appearance of a thickened dumb-bell with flattened ends and

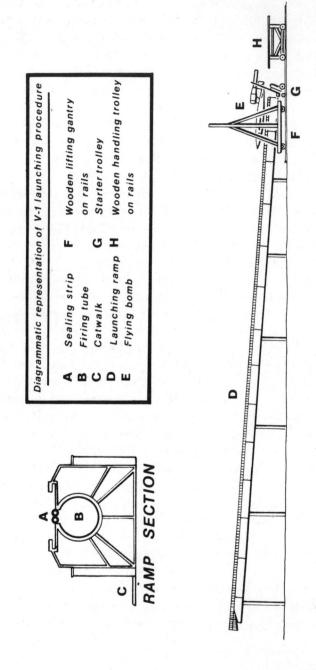

Diagrammatic representation of V-1 launching procedure

A Sealing strip   **F** Wooden lifting gantry
B Firing tube   on rails
C Catwalk   **G** Starter trolley
D Launching ramp   **H** Wooden handling trolley
E Flying bomb   on rails

RAMP SECTION

from the bar of which, near one extremity, protruded a lug
that stood up through the slot when the piston was in position.

This lug engaged the 'C' section launching rail, already
described as being under the mid part of the bomb, after it
had been winched up and placed in the launching spot at the
lower end of the ramp. This rail under the missile was a metal
casting and fitted quite loosely over the lug projection which,
as it ran up the slot, forced open a tubular sealing strip rather
resembling a type of enormous domestic draught excluder.

To propel this piston forward required the services of a
small trolly bearing cylinders of '*T-stoff*', hydrogen peroxide,
and granules of the catalyst, potassium permanganate. When
these two were brought together, the former was chemically
decomposed by the latter and steam produced which was
conducted into the firing tube. The resultant pressure shot the
piston to the upper end of its tube, taking the bomb with it. At
the end, the bomb had reached a speed of about 150 m.p.h.
and was still accelerating under the thrust of its own motor
which had been started up when the trolly was connected.
Inclined on an upward course by the ramp, the missile and
piston parted company, the one, with any luck, climbing
away, the other to fly a considerable distance from the open
end of the tube to be retrieved, each site was issued with only
two, and used again. Personnel meanwhile, clad in rubber
boots and protective clothing washed the resultant deposit
from the track of the ramp with brooms.

Before launching, a missile was assembled and the wings
placed in position, an operation calling for no more than
sliding them over the tubular spar and tightening the spar
securing bolts by hand. After this the compass was 'swung' in
the manner already described and the controls set for the
journey. For this the altitude was set within the operating
limits of the height control which permitted nothing below 300
metres (about 980 feet) or above 2,500 metres (8,000 feet)
although few, if any, ever made the Channel crossing at
anything like that height. With the air log, or journey counter
set to run out over the target and the compass setting made,

the missile was ready for its one-way trip.

The means by which control was maintained across the Channel was relatively simple and was achieved by a modified Askania automatic pilot. This had several advantages over other forms of guidance in that being of a straightforward design it was capable of showing a robust resistance to the shock of launching and it was operated by compressed air. The basic movements were the normal ones associated with climb and dive by means of the elevators while the rudder looked after not only directional guidance but also roll correction. Since a gyroscope will, once spinning, remain with a vertical axis and its relative horizontal plane perfectly level, whatever position its mounting may assume, it was relatively simple for the pitch and turn of such an instrument to be translated into pneumatic signals. These were directed to one side or another of a piston, under the control of a valve capable of introducing the air pressure to one face while cutting it off from the other. This piston, in turn moved an operating rod to the control linkage.

Directional control was slightly less simple since it relied on the mechanical comparison between the actual alignment

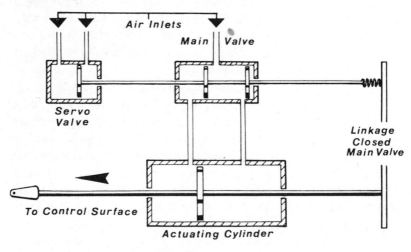

V-1 Control System

with the target set on the magnetic compass and the actual direction 'felt' by the gyro. Discrepancies between these two set in motion a motor, by means of a pair of switches, in such a way that the vertical control surface was moved until the two once more coincided. The actual thrust was applied to the operating rod and horn, once more, by a pneumatic servo-motor.

At the termination of a flight the air log operated a small guillotine which severed the pipeline to the rudder while another similarly chopped the tubes to the elevators so that no further movements could be passed to these control surfaces. At the same time, an electrical impulse was passed to a pair of small explosive charges inside the rear of the robot, but near to the inboard ends of the elevators: immediately these detonated they blew down a pair of spoilers, or small metal flaps under the tailplane. The area of these was enough to interrupt the air flow sufficiently to drop the nose of the bomb into a shallow diving position of about five degrees which, if the controls had operated at a great enough altitude would have become progressively steeper until it assumed the vertical. This seldom happened, however, the bombs tending to glide on occasion to their target, as even a relatively shallow angle of descent was enough to rob them of impulsion when the motor was starved of fuel.

Another design variation was the fitting of wooden wings and there seems to be some doubt as to whether these were confined to the later model with a reduced war-head and enlarged fuel capacity. On balance, it seems that this was not so as there are indications of metal wings being exchanged for wooden ones fairly early in the attacks. These wings, although retaining tips pressed from sheet steel, were otherwise of timber construction throughout and were consequently a little lighter in weight than their metal counterparts, tipping the scales at some 180 kilogrammes (395 pounds) as opposed to about 200 kilogrammes (445 pounds) when assembled on the steel spar. There were a few, however, which were carried on a rather heavier, drawn steel spar with a metal wing giving an increase in weight of 16 kilogrammes (30 pounds), all of which indicated that it was for reasons of economy, not performance considerations, that the modification was made so that only slight alterations in the centre of gravity took place which could be easily adjusted by an alteration of the spar position internally.

The covering of the timber wings was nothing more than ply while the ribs were cut from thicker laminations and pierced by circular lightening holes. A false spar at the root added robustness at the point of maximum stress.

It is worth mentioning that this longer-range version, which is more fully described in a later chapter, had its fuse pockets slightly differently arranged, being accessible still on the port side but at the horizontal mid-line of the war-head fairing. These fuses were of both mechanical and electrical type, the latter, designated ELAS 106 and ENT 106 were of a new and complex design which gave them high sensitivity. A short nose rod, with pressure-plate operation to make electrical contact on impact, ensured minimum penetration and therefore maximum blast effect.

At about the same time as the wooden wing was first encountered, it became evident that small changes were also taking place in the details of the automatic pilots, but after examination in this country it was decided that the modifications were much more likely to be for purposes of easier production than better performance.

Altogether it was manifestly evident at this period that the flying bomb was capable, if only to a limited degree, of improvement and this was being carried out. There followed speculation whether the air bottles, tested in their original form to about 3,500 pounds psi, would have to be replaced and whether the longer distances anticipated would call for better quality metal in the air intake valves, which had an operating life of only about thirty minutes, but there is no evidence that this was ever carried out.

Investigation of the recognizable parts, which were carefully collected from the scene of each flying bomb incident, caused some problems at first when what were obviously radio components were discovered; finally it was from the vicinity of an explosion in Antwerp that a near-complete example was obtained. This was contained in a small metal box, about eight inches square and plywood lined, carried in the rear of the fuselage behind the automatic pilot where it had a battery for powering both the tube filament and coding motor. This transmitter was of the S23E type with an LS50 tube wired as a Hartly oscillator with the high tension current of about 600 volts. The aerial was carried on take-off wound round a paxolin (impregnated paper) rod and in a tube of similar material and was drawn out in flight as described later. The actual coding unit consisted of a small electric motor, driving a paxolin coding wheel through a reduction gear, the coding characteristics being Morse. Since this was changed according to the launching area it was a simple matter for each to have its own code and be tracked by ordinary direction finding procedures. The frequency on which these instruments operated was something in the 500 kHz band and on the night of 19–20 June, monitoring services picked up three signals, on 438, 450 and 525 kHz which was the first intimation in this country of the operations of these.

Although the facility was never used, the war-head of a flying bomb could be used for the conveyance of a variety of poison gases, while experiments were at an advanced stage in fitting the Porsche L09-005 turbo-jet which would have given an improvement without recourse to such complications as the modification to springs etc. on the original motor, although, in point of fact the work along these lines was never completed.

In October 1944, the former *Erprobungskommando* Wachtel, which had retained its commanding officer when re-named Flak Regiment 155(W) on taking up operational duties, was again given a change of title, this time to that of the 5th Flak Division, still under Max Wachtel and retaining the deception that it was an anti-aircraft unit. Indeed, it seems that at this time much thought was given to security in the belief that the operations were the preoccupation of a vast army of Allied agents. To deceive these, such elaborate measures were adopted as fitting Argus impulse units on trucks and running them at sites far distant from the actual launching areas in order to 'draw off' the spies, while damaged sites were left *in situ* and decoys even assembled to add to the deception. These were not the only problems with which Flak Regiment 155 had to contend, for, at one point, Flieger Regiment 93 was withdrawn and the guard duties and those of site defence, which they were supposed to perform, had to be carried out by the Flak Regiment personnel, while at the same time launching the missiles, installing some of the equipment and in some measure preparing and maintaining the sites.

The actual number of 'Cherrystones' built by Fieseler *Werke* was small, being no more than 300 in all, but the robot was widely sub-contracted by such centres as Bruns *Werke* and Neidersachswerfen's *Mittelwerke*, the 'MT' of rocket component fame, while an assembly line capable of producing 5,000 per month was planned at the Volkswagen works at Fallersleben, and there was a similar assembly plant, underground at Nordhausen. These should have been capable of producing bombs in sufficient quantity to bombard the camps, troops and ship concentrations for which it was intended before the dawn of D-day and Operation 'Overlord' had it not been for the difficulties already outlined and the frequent setbacks from the attentions of the RAF's Bomber Command and their United States counterparts. As a result, instead, the missile was flung against the towns and villages surrounding London, in Surrey, Kent and Essex and at greater distances too where it inflicted something like one tenth of all the civilian casualties of the entire war.

3 | Laid Bare

The silent, secret war against the dangers of the so-called 'secret weapons' had been going on for the duration of hostilities, and even before. Small items of information had filtered in to London from a vast variety of sources: workers from the Nazi-occupied territories who kept their eyes open; men and women of the Polish underground who heard that a tanker driver maybe, had noticed tell-tale scorch marks, or perhaps low, circular exhaust vents at the back of a new building, and then risked their lives to obtain confirmation, all this and much more had been passed to London and carefully assembled and set beside the clues which could be gleaned from radio broadcasts which were monitored ceaselessly. But one of the drawbacks of attempting to assemble such a mighty jigsaw puzzle is that you may have the parts of several all mixed and be ignorant of the fact, so, sooner or later, it becomes vital to confirm what has been gathered with practical investigation which means, in the twentieth century, the use of cameras.

However, it occasionally comes about that Fate seems to take a helping hand and guide investigations, first for one side and then for the other and it was one of these lucky accidents which took place in 1942.

By this period of the conflict it was known that the Nazis had been conducting experiments with a type of small flying bomb, propelled by means of a rocket, a rather beautiful, tailless machine which may have been guided by radio, with a span in the region of five metres and narrow, slightly swept-back wings which reminded one of a glider. However thoughts about this type of thing would have been far from the

41

mind of Flight Lieutenant Steventon on 15 May when he was returning from a routine flight in a photographic Spitfire over Kiel. His return was via the western Baltic in order to photograph Swinemünde. Not far from the River Peene which gives its name to the village close at hand, he noticed signs of constructional work below and exposed a few frames of film to cover this. What he could not know was that he had preserved on record the first sightings of the experimental station which was to see, only seven months later, the launching of a prototype flying bomb of the type which was to bombard London two years hence and the first launching of the rocket, later to be known as the V-2, on 3 October, only 141 days after the photograph was taken. In the event, the single set of prints which resulted from the chance exposure could make little difference to the information already to hand of the activities in the long-range bombardment field by the enemy, since photographic intelligence is based to a large extent on comparison of pictures taken over a period. But it was known that the state of these weapons' development was such that the formation of a special committee, later to be known as the Flying Bomb Counter Measures Committee, was justified, under the chairmanship of Mr (now Lord) Duncan Sandys, who immediately brought to top priority the whole question of further investigation of the threat. Several officers were specially appointed to the work in addition to four interpreters to comb the results of photographic reconnaissance further, missions now being specially mounted for this purpose from the PRU headquarters at Benson, the work being shared by its American counterpart at Mount Farm.

There were four such sorties over the Baltic station in June 1942 alone, those on the second day of that month and that on 23 June when Flight Sergeant Peek took over a camera-equipped Mosquito, being especially useful since both days were blessed with bright sunshine.

Military intelligence is very rarely the result of work by one team working in a single sphere and this was the case in the search for Nazi secret weapons, since it was due to word passed to London from the occupied French coastal area that photographic aircraft were sent to cover the Calais vicinity in July. With the information now piling up that something sinister was taking place in northern France connected with the activities on the Baltic coast, the decision was swiftly taken to mount Operation 'Hydra'. Five hundred and ninety bombers were flung at Peenemünde in the late summer of 1943 while, ten days after this, the United States Air Force dealt with the areas near Calais at a critical time when the concrete of the bunkers was still setting. So great was the devastation that the now-hardened cement caused over the destroyed field that further intelligence reports indicated that the area was completely abandoned and work begun afresh some distance away.

As the year ripened into November a further piece of the massive jigsaw was offered by a contact on the ground who had kept his eyes open when in the Abbeville district. He had spotted a new and different type of building under construction at eight sites where he had been directed to work. Only a matter of days later a photographic sortie confirmed that these buildings existed and presented a very peculiar form in that they extended for something a little under 300 feet in length but had one end curved giving the structure the appearance of a gigantic hockey-stick laid on the ground or as one intelligence officer put it "like skis".

It quickly became obvious that these buildings had nothing to do with rockets; these were known to be some forty feet in length and to manoeuvre one round the curve would, although not impossible, have been a difficult and time-consuming undertaking. Clearly then, this seemed to indicate that the buildings were supplied to service a comparatively small weapon: perhaps not a rocket at all but a flying bomb.

This new turn in the chain of events was immediately presented to the committee over which Mr Duncan Sandys presided, a distinguished gathering which, after an adjournment to allow the latest estimate of the number of these erections to be made, was electrified when the total was stated to be twenty-six. This figure had increased to ninety-five, some directed towards Bristol and Plymouth, at the end of November when, in Great Britain, responsibility for the counter-measures was passed to the Air Staff.

One theory, which was examined, that the structures were storage sheds for rocket parts, was discarded when further study showed on one set of photographs twin lines of cement discs which could be the foundations for a series of uprights. To the trained interpreter this could only mean one thing, they marked the line of a long ramp up which something was to be fired, something small which would pass through the comparatively small doorways which could be seen; the case for a miniature aeroplane of some type was now becoming stronger, and this could only mean a flying bomb, but at this time no one had any idea what it looked like and photographs seemed to be of no assistance on this question, a perplexing state of affairs helped not at all by the silence on the subject from workers across the Channel.

On 28 November 1943 a new set of photographs was to hand from the cameras of Squadron Leader Merifield's Mosquito and they were fair. At first they appeared to show little that was new at the Peenemünde site but something in them caused the WAAF officer who had been checking earlier prints, to compare them with the new set. The girl in question was Flight Officer Babington Smith. She was the daughter of Sir Henry Babington Smith, former Private Secretary to the Viceroy of India and in consequence came from a background of firm dedication to serving one's country; but the service she was about to perform was dictated by chance rather than conscious effort. The first of the new run just included within its margin what she hoped to find, a long thin shape of the same length and width as those dimensions calculated for the support foundations in the French photographs: at last, confirmation that it was as suspected, a ramp: but better was to come for, on the end of this one was a minute cruciform shape, almost invisible to the untrained eye: a miniature aeroplane! Temporarily, they called it Peenemünde 20.

44

With the mass of photographs by now available it was relatively simple to calculate the time which these sites took to construct complete with their perplexing long buildings with curved ends, now recognized as storage sheds for flying bomb components. Briefed with this knowledge and after consultations with civil building advisers it was possible to estimate when the more advanced of these would be ready for use and when the attack by the new weapons might commence. It came out as a chillingly short period, no more than six weeks.

In so short a time it was obvious that a daylight mission was indicated and consequently responsibility for the attacks was passed to the American Eighth Air Force based in Great Britain which had gained something of a reputation for specialization in this type of work. Consequently, the first of these missions was mounted towards the end of December when the United States bombers attacked twenty-four of the bunker systems and the RAF five more, dropping the first of what was to be a total of 23,196 tons of high explosive on the targets. It was not long before the whole system of anticipated launching points was in a state of complete chaos and it was obvious that the first round had been won by Great Britain and America because, although clearly some of the long storage sheds had survived, albeit in a gravely damaged form, it was perfectly possible for flying bombs to be sent off without these, so it was the destruction of the actual ramps which mattered most.

What was not known at the time was that, so confident were the Nazis that flying bombs provided a chance to snatch victory out of impending defeat, that thousands of construction workers who had been engaged on the erection of defences against the anticipated invasion of the Continent by the Allies had been transferred to the building of launching areas for the new weapons. This fact had to be explained away as an "administrative muddle" in order not to make nonsense of such directives as that issued by the Führer who stated in Number 51, issued almost simultaneously with the transfer,

"The enemy must not be allowed to maintain a foothold on the coast, but must be thrown back into the sea at once. The coast in fact must be held in all circumstances, and all withdrawal is forbidden."

By the beginning of 1944 further reconnaissance over the districts of Picardy, Normandy and Artois seemed to show that work on the majority of the sites had been abandoned. True, some still showed signs of activity and received further attention from the RAF but this seeming industry was in fact openly carried on so that these, always vulnerable, sites would act as a decoy and divert British attention from new work which was first reported to London by underground workers as early as February. This indicated that a new, and much simplified system of launching ramps was under construction.

The form these took was of minimal construction consisting of a ramp, concrete roads, compass swinging base and a small cluster of only the most essential buildings some of which were disguised as farm outhouses or even hayricks, while others were of simple construction and consisted of only logs and earth. It was April 1944 before the first of these was discovered and they demonstrated the degree of thought which had gone into the planning. Firstly, intelligence sources in the field told that now only German and convict labour was being employed, evidence that the many subterfuges of slave labour, an excess of sand in mixed concrete for example, had achieved the desired effect on their Nazi masters. Secondly, the layout was arranged to make maximum use of the natural cover to be gained from the wooded areas where the launching ramps were now situated while, thirdly, they were set out with the minimum of spread so that, even once discovered, they were individually very difficult targets to attack from the air.

Even so, the urgency of the situation was such that some of the twelve modified sites which were discovered in quick succession during April were picked out to be the target for a new assault to take place on 13 April. This was unusual in that it was to be delivered by fighter-bombers and the Spitfire 9s of 602 and 132 Squadrons of the RAF had been picked for

Cumulative weight of attack on V-weapon sites per ten thousand tons of bombs dropped.

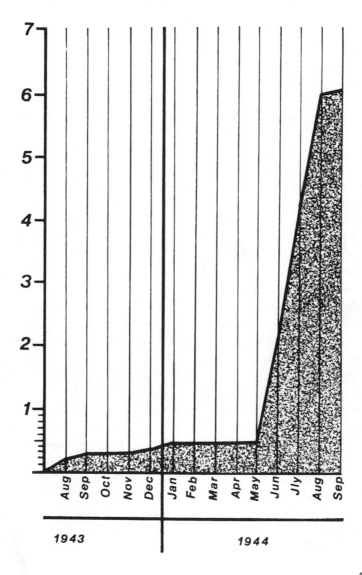

7

6

5

4

3

2

1

Aug Sep Oct Nov Dec Jan Feb Mar Apr May Jun Jly Aug Sep

1943   *1944*

the experimental work. Training for use against such small, compact targets as these had been carried out over the bombing range at Llanbedr, on the coast of North Wales as recently as the middle of the previous March and had immediately shown that the accurate placing of a 500-pound bomb was not without difficulty. The bomb was carried centrally under the belly so that, if the aircraft was dived almost vertically, releasing the load only flung the explosive into the revolving propeller, while approaching the target at something like forty-five degrees brought problems with aiming.

During the three weeks spent in experimental drops it was discovered that the best way to solve the problem called for an approach to the target at a height of 12,000 feet until the target appeared below. Each pilot then individually dived down to an altitude of 3,000 feet, flattened out and after a three-second pause, pulled the bomb release. Once this method was perfected and a reasonable degree of accuracy obtained, the two squadrons returned to Detling where they joined the Royal Australian Air Force's 453 Squadron which had already gained some experience in this type of attack on 'No-ball' targets, as the launching areas were code named, during March when perhaps some of the decoys and less heavily damaged bunker type sites came in for attention.

There had been a similar attack on the previous day but 13 April was to be the baptism of fire in the new work for 602 and 132 Squadrons which were to attack the ramp and firing point at Bouillancourt which lies some 20 kilometres (12 miles) south of Le Tréport. As it turned out, the strike was fairly uneventful and the twenty-four machines dropped their bombs with little interference from the defences.

By now, a definite pattern could be made out in the arrangement of the sites. It consisted of nine areas of which four were aligned against London with the remainder variously directed towards Brighton, Dover, Newhaven, Southampton, Portsmouth, Bristol and Plymouth. Within each of these sectors British Intelligence had given each of the

'No-ball' targets identification numbers with the result that the launching site for flying bombs at Ailly-le-Vieux-Clocher became 'No-ball 27' for example.

Attacking these targets imposed a considerable mental strain on the pilots brought about by the degree of concentration called for coupled with the fact that some of the sites by now enjoyed a reputation for defence by fearsome and well-directed anti-aircraft fire. In addition, the physical punishment which the pilots suffered could result in such symptoms as internal haemorrhage and ruptures.

These then, were the sort of additional hazards which faced the men of 132 Squadron, the cosmopolitan 602 Squadron which included Australian, British, Canadian, French and New Zealand pilots on its strength, and 453 Squadron when they took off from Detling at 12.25 p.m. on 16 April and set course for the forest of Crécy where their target was the heavily-defended ramp and bunkers at Ligercourt. Backed up by the defences at Abbeville, the guns in the immediate vicinity were a selection, numbering about thirty in all, of 88 mm, 27 mm and 20 mm calibre. Crossing the French coast at 10,000 feet, the pilots quickly identified their target and went down in turn to 3,000 feet to release their bombs through a hail of fire from the defences. Once free of the weight of their loads, the pilots hauled on their controls and made altitude as quickly as possible still pursued by the deadly fire which claimed more than one Spitfire to add to the holocaust below.

After a move of base to Ford, the squadrons of 125 Wing continued this type of mission throughout May, often delivering more than one attack on different targets in a single day. Other squadrons also joined this type of work now concentrated almost entirely on the modified sites which, although small and well camouflaged, stood a greater chance of being successfully dealt with, but even so, the success of this form of assault was mixed, as witness that by fighter-bombers on 27 May which achieved little on an area which later proved to be an experimental flying-bomb installation.

While this sort of thing was going on, the regular

49

photographic missions continued and, from the new prints coming in, it emerged that some sites were being taken only so far and then seemingly abandoned after the concrete had been laid. At first the logical solution to this in the minds of British Intelligence was that there was some delay in the delivery of supplies. However, this proved not to be the case for it became evident that to judge from photographs taken at regular intervals of a flying-bomb training school, the sequence of construction meant that, once the foundations had hardened, the actual ramp and parts for the vital buildings were being delivered as prefabricated parts and assembled on the site. The implications of this discovery were grim in the extreme in that they indicated not only that areas hitherto deemed to be unworthy of continued attention could be made ready at short notice, but also that some of the less damaged bunkers for flying bombs on which no further work had been carried out, could be rapidly brought to operational standard; a position which was worsened after the Normandy landings when it was realized that the photographic aircraft would have their work cut out covering the areas in front of the Allied Armies and would therefore be able only to provide incidental coverage of flying-bomb installations for the time being. Happily this state of affairs was short-lived and photographic reconnaissance of the 'No-ball' areas was resumed after the first flood of activity in connection with the Normandy landings was over and five days after the first troops had established the initial bridgeheads the sites were again covered on 11 June. It was just in time; under a dozen of these had not been looked at since before the dawn of D-day and it was evident that something was afoot. It had been arranged that at the first sign of anything of this sort the codeword 'Diver' would be signalled to alert all the defences that attack was imminent. It scarcely called for a second check that this was no isolated work on a few ramps but a concentrated effort to prepare them all for use. The same evening that the photographs had been taken, Wing Commander Douglas Kendall at RAF Station, Medmenham, passed the codeword which had been awaited for so long and those who received it braced themselves for the unknown.

Despite the depressing list of possible secret weapons which Dr Jones had submitted at the outbreak of war, there was a tendency to think in singular terms when the most likely form which the new menace would take was being sought. This may have been partly due to the Nazis themselves who frequently broadcast sinister references to "a secret weapon", thus giving the impression that only one was in course of development and the remainder had probably not progressed beyond a design or prototype stage; consequently most people among the Allies believed the weapon would be a rocket although there were those who found it difficult to believe an explosive-carrying missile of this type was at all feasible.

Somewhat later it became obvious that some sort of robot aeroplane was also envisaged but any jubilation which may have been felt in Great Britain when the American B-17 bombers struck at the hardening concrete structures at Watten, near Calais, already described, was technically misplaced for, unknown at the time of the attack on 27 August, the bunker system was in fact designed for rockets and not flying bombs. Although in the long run this may have appeared to be of little consequence, it was in fact something of a dissipation of effort as the only wholly satisfactory way to combat the threat was a maximum effort against the weapon which was likely to be used first and the fact was now beginning to emerge that this was most likely to be "an air mine with wings" or "aerial torpedo" as it was variously described at the time.

This confusion between the pair of most immediately likely weapons was inadvertently helped by reports reaching Britain from neutral sources. Typical was that from Stockholm a little later, at a time when "secret weapon descriptions" were being passed in abundance through European capitals. It spoke of a "flying rocket bomb", thus anticipating the V-3 described in a later chapter, which was towed into the air by a conventional aeroplane and finally released a few miles from the target. It was then, so the story ran, automatically sent to an altitude of about five miles with the aid of a special rocket. From the top of this trajectory it glided under radio control to its target where it exploded with a blue and orange flame which "hung in the air for some time afterwards". Ignoring just how a flame could do this, the report concluded with a note that the destruction within a radius of 400 yards was "colossal" and, in the spirit of a film 'trailer', added that it would be tried out first on the Russian Front before being sent against Britain.

However, nonsense such as this could not be dismissed at the time and had to be carefully compared with reports from agents in France and Germany but in the last analysis the only practical access to what was going on was via the results of photographic reconnaissance. The chance exposures which Flight Lieutenant Steventon had made over the Baltic coast were perhaps the real beginnings of this because questions were raised in the minds of interpreters by the sight of circular embankments. These were later mentally linked with reports of weapon trials at the end of the year and with reports obtained through Norway, more credible than the subsequent ones already described, which spoke, as early as the third quarter of 1939, of experiments with some form of rocket-assisted artillery.

With these and other fragmentary reports, it became possible at the beginning of 1943 to forecast the possible means of launching and range of such a weapon, while the size of the war-head was deduced as knowledge of the construction was built-up; that splendid Scientific Intelligence Officer, Dr R.V. Jones even accurately estimating at a later date the likely production rate and number held in stock.

Further aerial watch on the experimental station at Peenemünde indicated that the perplexing rings were still in use, but these were not immediately connected with rocket missiles because one school of thought believed that an extremely long ramp would be called for to aim them with any degree of accuracy. Alternatively it was suggested that rockets could be launched from underground bases which would reveal only circular openings to photographic 'eyes'. There too, interpreters were instructed to look in addition for something approximating to the "flying rocket bomb" which Stockholm had described and perhaps an updated version of the 'Big Bertha' gun which had shelled Paris at a range of 76 miles (122 kilometres) from Coucy exactly twenty-five years and one month before.

This vigilance quickly paid dividends and after informed study of further photographs it was decided that the circular embankments could be nothing other than rocket test stands. With a new set of prints of Peenemünde taken at the beginning of the following June, new problems were set, however, the principal of these being the use for a column or tower about twice the height of an average house, their appearance probably explaining the later code name 'Big Ben'.

These pictures were augmented later that month during a sortie carried out in ideal lighting conditions and it was these at last which showed what had been sought so long, for, lying horizontally on a pair of low-loader vehicles was a pair of rockets.

The use of these *Meillerwagen* opened up a new train of thought at RAF Medmenham because it had hitherto been assumed that dimensions such as these would preclude the movement of rockets by anything other than railways, a theory which seemed to be confirmed by the complex of lines at the Baltic base. Indeed, working on the assumption that any concentrated attack by rockets would have to come from northern France, a careful watch was being kept on this area with successive flights of photographic Spitfires for any sign that railway spurs were about to be laid which would indicate that launching areas, the idea of launching *pads* still lay in the future, were being prepared. It was not long before just such workings were found over a large part of the Pas de Calais and the Somme where cuttings were being gouged through high ground, trees felled in preparation for ground levelling and massive areas of concrete laid. Yet none of these indications seemed to fit any pattern, known or theoretically decided, a state of affairs which was to be explained later when it was known that the activities were not directed to the establishment of bases for any one weapon but for several, including flying bombs.

In the late autumn of 1942, Duncan Sandys sifted the complete dossier of accumulated information, which had been presented to him over several months and decided that the menace was sufficiently great for some effort to be made to arrive, as far as possible, at firm conclusions about what was actually going on. Since this could only be decided in the light of the newest visual information, a complete new reconnaissance of the entire vicinity of the workings was ordered, involving hundreds of photographs resulting from a staggering number of special missions from Benson RAF Station and with some American assistance, each one flown alone in a swift, polished and specially blue-camouflaged machine without armament of any sort. In the event, this mass of material proved of only routine value in the search for rocket bases, although the effort was far from wasted in that it was these which gave the first sight of the odd, curved-end structures which were to prove a large piece of evidence in the assembly of flying bomb data. Indeed, Christmas had passed, the cold winds of March were trying the windows and doors of the mock-Tudor mansion of Danesfield where the Photographic Interpretation Unit worked overlooking the Buckinghamshire Thames between Henley and Marlow, when, to this opulent grey stone building, there was passed from London an item of information to the effect that in the south-east of Poland, near the isolated village of Blizna, rockets had supposedly been seen in clearings cut in the marsh-surrounded forests. This was obviously the type of work for which the photographic Mosquito was admirably suited and one was immediately despatched to check on the report, not from England but from Italy in order to reduce the flying time over enemy territory. But, as is so often the way, the prints showed nothing of value, since the chances of finding a rocket in the open were small. Even so, a second sortie was ordered about eight weeks later and the swiftly-developed film showed that this time the flight had been crowned with success, for there was a rocket at last, not alone but loaded on its road vehicle: confirmation at last that sites could well be set up without any of the preliminary clues of track-laying and earth movement.

Useful as this discovery was, it did no more than confirm what was already suspected and added nothing to the frequently-asked questions of when attacks from the stratosphere were likely to begin and even if such a bombardment was possible. The authorities were becoming gravely concerned, London and the Home Counties were already under attack by flying bombs and guests noted that the subject of the fresh weapon crept increasingly into the conversation round Churchill's luncheon table. It was then that Wing Commander Kendall took the decision that the whole of the now considerable coverage of Peenemünde and the French Channel coast must be re-checked, a massive undertaking which fell to only two men.

The re-examination had been going on for some time when one of the early prints showing the foreshore with the great sweep of earthworks on the Baltic came under scrutiny. There it was exactly as before and as unhelpful as ever, the great area of asphalt, the heaped earth, the odd-looking tower about three storeys high ... odd looking tower?! They looked again. It was no tower but a rocket, set upright on its fins: no launching tube; no bunkers; no rail links. So that was how it was to be done. The vital piece in the puzzle had been found. No need for anything but a simple pad and flame deflector and a road vehicle which could be simply hidden under the trees, it was going to be difficult, extremely difficult, but at last they knew what to look for.

The codeword for these gropings in the dark had been 'Bodyline' but after the more specific track of events became obvious this had been suspended in favour of 'Crossbow', a wide term which also included all the counter-measures for the new armoury, and work continued under this heading after it was established that the first of the attacks was to be by means of the flying bomb. But in the event, neither the new title nor the new discovery seemed to invoke any increased blessing for the work of laying bare the Nazi secrets. Many hundreds of hours in the air over enemy territory and the exposure of a great quantity of film had managed only twice to discover suspicious clearings.

In order to remedy this state of affairs a complex set of orders was issued in an attempt to devise a system whereby the source of the launchings could be discovered; the first of these anticipating the later difficulties as shown by its date of origin, 23 April 1944. In this the assumed targets were, in addition to the obvious one of Number 42 London, Bristol, Portsmouth and Southampton.

The detection of the launching points was to be of prime importance so that 'Big Ben' counter-measures could be advanced and to do this it was planned to modify the radar stations at Swingate, Rye, Pevensey, Poling and Ventnor in 11 Group and those of 10 Group at Branscombe, Ringstead and Southbourne, which with the pair at St Lawrence and Newchurch were to combine in a special watch. This was intended also to be the means of giving some level of warning to the general public.

Described by the codeword 'Firework', the procedure for determining the first took the form of a requirement that the supervisor at any of the radar stations should pass, via a special circuit to a scientific observer at 11 Group's filter room "all data obtained regarding the origin and flight of enemy rockets". To this end, a buzzer was installed by means of which the scientific observer could be called if absent from his office. In the event of failure to contact him, the information was to be passed to the duty officer.

Army information from sound ranging units was similarly passed by means of a special telephone line to one of the two battery headquarters which took responsibility for informing the scientific observer's keyboard as was data obtained by flash recording, priority being given when the information was prefixed by the codewords 'Popgun', in a similar manner to the use of 'Firework', which was then followed by the individual code for the site, the same code as that employed by the radar stations being used to preface any information other than that announcing the actual discharge of a missile.

A reciprocal system also operated whereby the scientific observer could inform the sound ranging battery headquarters at Canterbury when a rocket had been fired, adding an estimate if possible of the area from which it seemed to appear.

Situated at the General Headquarters, Home Forces, the duty group captain was also supplied with this information as well as making use of his contact with the Home Security War Room, thus briefed he was responsible for passing the intelligence to a long list of officers and stations which included such widely divergent contacts as the controller at RAF Benson, the Air Ministry; the Admiralty; the United States Eighth Air Force; Bomber Command, RAF; the watch officer at Medmenham (via Benson) and the Headquarters of Air Defence of Great Britain and that of the Second Tactical Air Force, "with" concluded the document, "an essential element of speed".

Other orders followed, of which perhaps the most significant were those of 30 August which struck a more positive note; the atmosphere of vague hopefulness was gone and in its place was one of determination speaking for the first time of counter-measures and "defeat of the enemy's intention". Pilots were to be kept fully briefed on the day to day situation; aircrews were to be instructed to be especially vigilant when in the vicinity of rocket launching areas and, most importantly, 11 Group was to despatch, at least twice a day, armed fighter reconnaissance sorties over the forward storage depots and their associated road and rail communications. One of these missions was directed to be carried out in the evening and transport movement was to be immediately attacked, responsibility for this outside the radius of 11 Group being taken by the Tactical Air Force. Two additional sorties were to be made during the hours of darkness by Intruder aircraft.

During daylight, two wings of Spitfires for use as a striking force had to be kept at thirty minute readiness, a role from which they could be released only by Headquarters of the Allied Air Force, release which would be granted only should the Spitfires be required to assist as a matter of urgency the day bombers which were supporting the armies in France, the RAF units detailed for anti-flying-bomb work being pressed into service against rocket launching activities if this permission was granted.

By night, there was now similar positive thinking in the spirit of striking back and three Mosquito 6 machines, which had up to that time been used against flying bombs by 418 Squadron from Hunsdon and a further trio of similar aircraft from 605 Squadron, hitherto similarly employed from Manston were to be kept for despatch against rocket launching activity at half an hour's notice.

The next set of orders appeared shortly after, on 17 September and opened with a note that the launching sites were in Holland, adding that henceforth every counter-measure was to be taken to detect the bases and then destroy them. Chief among these was one unexpectedly situated in The Hague's Haagsche Bosch, the large, partly-wooded area of the park providing the forward storage area. The whereabouts of rocket sources such as this and the similar one to which the Nazis retreated on nearby Duindigt Racecourse when the advancing armies drove them from the first were revealed by sources on the ground, now much more active and as much a part of the comprehensive network designed to bare the secrets of the new weapon as were the Service Intelligences.

By this time a small change had taken place in the arrangements for counter-measures in that these were now the responsibility of 12 Group with an original provision that the

Fighter commitment be met by the Coltishall Sector by Tempest 5s from 3, 56, and 486 Squadrons at Matlask, 80 and 274 from Coltishall itself and Spitfire 9s of 229 Squadron also based there. But the exigencies of the immediate demands from the Continent made this an impractical arrangement and amendment was swiftly made to provision that Air Defence of Great Britain should "indicate from time to time Squadrons which are available".

The mobile nature of a portion of the Nazi rocket launching force continued to pose problems throughout even this later period and the value of the work of the PRUs has already been made clear. In the spring of 1945 this work was being performed for 12 Fighter Group by the camera-equipped Spitfires from 26 Squadron. This type of machine had been responsible for a large part of the photographic surveillance which had made possible the degree of preparedness for the attacks by the V-weapons. The flight to Blizna has already been described and called for a Mosquito of 60 Photographic Reconnaissance and Decoy Squadron, South African Air Force, piloted by Captain Pienaar to make the journey to Poland from San Severo but no mention has yet been made of the identity of the squadrons, also equipped with Mosquito PR4s, which took many of the first photographs of Peenemünde. Initial work was carried out by Number 540 which had been formed in October 1942 at Leuchars in Scotland. In covering the launching sites in France, Mosquitos were again used, this time by 140 Squadron. At this period 400 and 544 Squadrons at home were flying Spitfires for this type of work, the former also using Mustangs as did 4 Squadron until the beginning of 1944 when they too took on Spitfire 11s which at first were augmented by some Spitfire 13s and Mosquito 16s. The cameras of all the single seaters were of the oblique pattern while the twin engined machines had, for the most part, cameras in vertical mountings; there were exceptions, however, an example of oblique photography in a Mosquito being the Mark 16 in which Flight Lieutenant Adcock attempted to cover the

Watten site in August 1944. This particular machine had an oblique camera, arranged to face forward, on one of the wing-mounted external fuel tanks, thus marking something of a change of role for the type which is usually associated with high-level reconnaissance. But, whatever method was used, sufficient has been said here to show how valuable this branch of RAF work could be; work in which it was supported by United States pilots flying for the most part Lockheed P-38F Lightnings or later, Northrop P-61 Black Widows, in uncovering the secrets of what was to be an entirely new type of warfare. But all this skill expended by the pilots, processers, interpreters and photographic specialists, not forgetting the men who laboured long hours in blacked-out hangars to keep the machines in airworthy condition, would have been of considerably less value had it not been for the wide spectrum of skills combined in the Allied Intelligence Services; yet even these were reliant to some extent on the work of the men and women 'in the field' the most audacious of whom must surely be the members of the Polish Home Army who, according to that indefatigable collector of espionage facts and prolific writer in the fields of both fact and fiction on the subject, Bernard Newman, salvaged test examples flown without war-heads, of both a V-1 and a V-2 in the Sarnaki district on the River Bug. The first they secreted in a lake, the second at a disused airfield from which the dismantled parts were flown under cover of darkness in an RAF Dakota sent for the purpose from Italy, the final moments of departure being fraught with spine-chilling danger when the heavily-laden transport stuck twice in the soft ground before finally getting away.

4 | Codeword 'Diver'

"Enemy Flying Bombs will be referred to or known as 'Diver' aircraft or pilotless planes."

SECRET DEFENCE INSTRUCTION

The reactions of the Finch family were typical of the attitude of the general public under the fresh form of attack but 'their' bomb (another fell on the identical spot on 29 July) of 16 June was not among the first to fall on southern England. The attack had opened initially three days earlier on 13 June following massive work begun immediately after the first Allied landings to complete at least some of the unfinished launching sites.

To mark the opening of the new Battle of London, Colonel Wachtel had taken it upon himself to make a speech, to the officers and men who would be delivering the new attack, twenty-four hours before the first launch and then no effort was spared to prepare for the first of what was confidently hoped in Nazi circles would be 500 per day. In fact only ten were launched of which six failed to reach the English coast. The defenders knew nothing of this fiasco, however, and the long-awaited 'Diver' machinery was immediately set into motion.

The first pair of flying bombs was actually logged by one of the auxiliary coastguards at Folkestone, Kent, Frederick C. Marsh BEM who had recorded them as "two aircraft with lighted cockpits coming in from the French coast in a north-westerly direction".

The post which this officer manned was situated at the end of Folkestone Harbour so that it jutted out well into the sea but it naturally fell to a post of 1 Group, Royal Observer Corps to send the first warning of the bomb's approach over land. The time was 4.06 a.m. when the two observers at Post Mike 2 covering Dymchurch, noted the sound of a strange aircraft approaching from some eight miles out to sea; immediately identified and reported to the operations room, it crashed twelve minutes later near Gravesend. The second bomb fell shortly after, on a railway viaduct at Bethnal Green, where it claimed the lives of six people, injured nine and others and blocked all the lines out of Liverpool Street Station. Whether it had completed its journey will probably never be known for there is some evidence to support the claim that it had fallen to anti-aircraft fire since the fuse of a heavy shell was found in the wreckage.

These early bombs were observed by a small number of Junkers 88s which followed at some distance, a fact which caused some uncertainty in the minds of the defenders as to what was actually being attempted and it is on record that in one area the public 'alert' was sounded twice with an intermediate 'raiders passed' in a very short space of time. Further example of the confusion lies in the fact that no less than twenty-two were confidently reported before dawn, the remaining pair of the opening quartet falling harmlessly in open country. Perhaps the greatest impact of these first flying bombs was that made by the sound which, based on the crude pulse-jet principle, lacked the smooth note of the modern jet and was described in such terms as "Like a Model-T Ford going up a hill", by an observer or "Like a motor-bike with a two-stroke engine", by an artillery sergeant who added that it was "something black trailing a strong flame" as it came in over the sea.

With two wasted, one in Kent and one in Sussex, and only limited loss of life and property, the opening of the attack had been inauspicious, a situation made all the more foolish by the lull in future operations brought about by a shortage of flying bombs. However by 11.18 p.m. on 15 June this had been put right and with the order "Open fire on Target 42" the first of the 150 or so which were to be sent off in the next twenty-four hours was on its way to London. The salvoes which followed, made their way through a light rain which persisted until after the first launchings ceased at 4.30 a.m., although in some parts of southern England witnesses to the flight of the first bomb which was to crash at 11.40 p.m. still describe it as "a beautiful night".

Shortly after this, the Nazis went so far as to record a running commentary on the launching procedure describing how

> The explosive weapons lie in the depth of a bunker. Spotlights spread a glaring light over the shining bodies of the ton-weights of the explosive missiles. They are waiting in a row behind one another. It looks like a slow-moving conveyor belt.
>
> The crews in their black overalls launch one missile after another. Each time a low buzzing breaks the silence. The missiles are on their way. Within a short time they cross the coast, smash through the A-A barrage and the defensive belt round the British capital and then fly on to London.

This graphic description fails to make mention that of the first group only seventy-three reached London or that eleven did not "smash through" the defences but were triumphantly shot down – on to the heads of the Londoners beneath. These guns were firing very low, one eyewitness remembers, so that, if they failed to bring a bomb down, civilians were almost in more danger from the rain of shell splinters.

Nearer in to London the cloud base was low that night and against the overcast the light from the propulsion units sent not only a glow over the sky but was also reflected on to the ground with a flickering, bright light which could be seen through the open doors of the outdoor 'Anderson' shelters making its seemingly inexorable path across familiar gardens. It was this light which was noted by many of the troops who were being brought into London that night for embarkation at the Surrey Docks but it was a sergeant in charge of a Home Guard picket after an unauthorized sojourn in the George who was among the most troubled, complaining that his vision was obscured by "little aeroplanes with a light up their arse". He was relieved the following morning to discover that they were material and not the product of an excess of alcohol!

By Friday, 16 June there had been some improvement in the weather with a smoother Channel, better visibility and a clearing sky with a light west-north-west wind. Still uncertain what was happening people had gone to work that morning with the 'raiders passed' siren unsounded and one such worker, employed in the Experimental Design Office of Hawker Aircraft evacuated to Claremont House, Esher from Kingston-on-Thames did not have his first experience of one of these missiles until this time. Of course warning leaflets had been issued some while before announcing the threat, but perhaps it was too far in the past for, the young man as he hurried to work at 8.30 a.m., found himself thinking that the sound which was so unfamiliar came from the motors of Junkers 52/3m troop carriers with parachutists attempting to stage a counter-invasion with a drop of armed men into nearby Richmond Park, and once again he remembers the sound as of that from a two-stroke motor cycle. That lunch time the majority of the draughtsmen and tracers came out on to the grass in front of the house to get a breath of fresh air and were suddenly aware of the strange noise again approaching from dead ahead. Very soon there came into view a flying bomb making straight for them from the south-east and while still a short distance from the assembly, the motor stopped. At this point in time unfamiliarity meant that the population had not yet associated the sudden silence with immediate dive and explosion so the group simply stood there and watched. As it happened this particular bomb glided out of their sight towards Staines and exploded in the distance behind them, but had it behaved in the manner of the majority and exploded within a short distance of the point where the motor cut out, the entire Hawker design staff would have been wiped out at a stroke!

Back at their drawing-boards, two of the party immediately began to put on paper what they had seen and, although there were discrepancies with regard to the jet unit, their estimates

(*Above*) The sight which greeted the Finch family and their neighbours after dawn

(*Below*) The same location thirty years later

"The sirens were still in position and maintained in working order but now largely silent"

Small brick-built surface shelter at the end of a suburban garden

A preserved specimen, still flying, of the de Havilland Mosquito which distinguished itself in both photographic and fighter roles during the operations against flying bombs

A Type 1 flying bomb immediately after launching

Part of a launching ramp, after capture, showing the end of the tube into which the piston fitted

The piston from a flying bomb launching catapult. At the top, the large lug engaged the underneath of the missile. Example displayed in IWM.

A Handley Page Halifax bomber over a heavily-bombed 'No-ball' site

The RAF's Avro Lancaster bomber employed to attack 'V' targets

Part of a formation of Boeing B-17G bombers of the United States Eighth Air Force set course for an attack on a 'No-ball' target

Admiral Sir Edward Evans (later Lord Mountevans) views the remains of a 'Morrison' table shelter

A policeman guarding the remains of houses at Shirley, Surrey, damaged during June 1944

A piece of flying bomb, measuring $6\frac{1}{2} \times 4\frac{1}{2}$ inches, found in August on a pavement in a suburb south of London

The wreckage of a flying bomb being piled up near to a barrage balloon the fins of which are deflated; the air at altitude and not the gas in the main envelope caused this as the balloon ascended

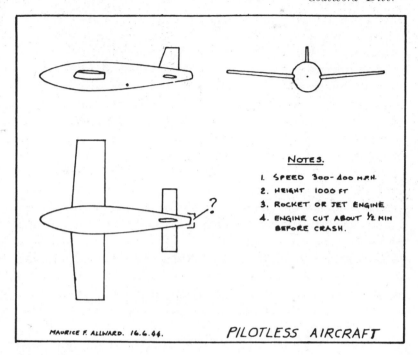

NOTES.

1. SPEED 300-400 M.P.H.
2. HEIGHT 1000 FT
3. ROCKET OR JET ENGINE
4. ENGINE CUT ABOUT ½ MIN BEFORE CRASH.

MAURICE F. ALLWARD. 16.6.64.

PILOTLESS AIRCRAFT

One of the drawings produced on 16 June after the first sight of a flying bomb over Claremont House, Esher

of size, speed and altitude agreed exactly. A telephone call by their superiors brought an official from the Ministry of Aircraft Production later in the afternoon to look at their work and he was able to confirm that their observations coincided exactly with what was already known of the new weapon.

It is interesting to speculate how many people owed their lives to the fact that the missile gave warning of imminent explosion by this cessation of sound, because this behaviour was unintentional and incidental to the design, being caused by the fuel splashing away from the feed pipe when the bomb assumed a certain angle, usually that of a dive.

Indeed there was no other explanation than this of the strange pranks which seemed to be played by some V-1s;

sometimes an engine would cut, only to restart and there were occasions when missiles would turn round and begin to steer a course back towards the Channel which they had so recently crossed. Indeed this type of thing some people found the most difficult to bear and Mrs Margaret Draper, then working as a telephone operator at Ashford Hospital, west of London, recalls the strain of this and never feeling entirely secure even after a bomb had passed despite the comparative safety of a claustrophobically sand-bagged operations room with the piled bags reaching above the top of the windows. The only attitude of mind to adopt, she found, and in this she was typical of many, was mentally to shrug off such sights as three bombs together in a small patch of sky and the chaos of death and destruction they sowed in the nearby streets, as quickly as possible and turn her thoughts to the work in hand. This was no callous approach – wedded only a short time to a commando, Margaret Draper knew all about war and its strains – but a defence mechanism which each person had to discover for him or herself.

The first complete day of the attacks found the total launchings placing a severe strain on the fifty-five sites available and the number of bombs sent over had risen only to 244 by the following Saturday. Of these the number which approached the coast was still somewhere in the ratio of those launched on the first day when six had been lost either due to failure to rise from the ramps or premature explosion in the air.

Despite all the benefits of a remarkable Intelligence Service there was no call for complacency and every item of information which could prove of assistance in meeting the missile was swiftly seized upon. Into this category came the drawings which were quickly turned out by two of the young draughtsmen who had so recently enjoyed such a remarkable escape and although both were vague about the exact details of the rear end and propulsion unit, the sketches were of sufficient accuracy to excite the attention of experts from London, who made a special journey to examine them and both men were pleased to discover that their estimate of speed and altitude at 300-400 m.p.h. and 1,000 feet (620 km/hr and 305 metres) respectively were remarkably accurate.

Looking at one of those drawings today, it is of interest to note two things, one is the laconic observation in the margin "Engine cut out about $\frac{1}{2}$ min before crash", the other is that the leading edge of the wings are drawn with a slight degree of sweep back. This poses the question even at this point in time of how many types there were. Certainly the most common was one with straight, untapered wings but the first, official drawings which appeared in the newspapers on the Wednesday following the opening of the main attack showed a '*Vergeltung 1*' with short, equally tapered wings and American Intelligence sources went so far as to quote dimensions for this type. Indeed, general observation went several points better than this and in time there appeared in the technical press a total of seven variants all based on "personal sightings", ranging from the accepted version, via a model with a very large wing span to one with a pair of diminutive elliptical mainplanes. The mystery is deepened by the unquestionable recollection of a man who had just this form drawn for him by a friend in chalk on the paving stones, long before this version was published in the Press!

Full details of this new type of warfare appeared in the national dailies on 17 June, some contenting themselves with such details as the facts that the missile was jet-propelled and the weight of explosive carried, while others were more helpful and included such hints "How to Avoid the Blast". The official advice began with the obvious instruction:

> If in the street go to a shelter if there is one very close. Take whatever substantial cover is available; if there is none, lie flat near – not against – a wall, and protect the head in any way possible. Avoid glass doors and windows.
>
> In your home use your shelter when danger is imminent. If it is not within reach duck under a table, get into an inner passage or under the stairs or behind a thick wall – always away from glass – and protect your face as much as you can.

It went on to describe how it was necessary to keep windows and skylights open day and night, pointed out that drawn curtains could give additional protection if they were sufficiently heavy and added that an old mattress against a window would protect the people in the room.

By this time many 'Morrison' shelters (named after the Minister of Home Security) had been issued. These were table-like constructions of steel for use indoors and, while doubling as an ordinary table, were strong enough to save the lives of persons underneath, who were additionally protected by stiff wire netting at the sides coming down to floor level. Many people made up beds under these and regularly slept there in order to get some sleep at all with the frequent 'alerts'. These shelters "should be placed" the official advice concluded, "out of the line of flying glass and protect it as much as possible with other solid furniture", adding as a seeming afterthought, "In shops take advantage of any cover provided by goods, counters, etc." The *Evening News* was even more helpful and went into details of the best position to adopt when danger was "imminent". After a warning to avoid making undue noise so that "your ears may give you warning" it told its readers to go down on their hands and knees and to tuck their head in. The reporter anticipated the question "What is imminent danger?" by admitting "The Home Security have no official definition of it", but, true to the time-honoured manner of government departments to talk their way out of anything and still preserve a verbal escape route for themselves added: "... it means when you hear a flying bomb – however distant – and have reasonable grounds for supposing you are on its path".

Today these gems of advice have a slightly comic ring and the phraseology seems prim, but at the time they were studied in grim earnest and as time went by one grew used to the sight of such worthy citizens as policemen suddenly flinging themselves into the gutter and perhaps joining them there, eye to eye at pavement level as a pilotless plane thundered overhead. There was nothing at all amusing about it in the summer of 1944. The situation was summed up by Mr Herbert Morrison when he told the House of Commons: "It is essential that there should be the least possible interruption to all work vital to the country's needs at this time".

But a popular daily paper in the same issue which reported these words, two days after the opening of the main attack, struck a more hopeful note with the headline "Pilotless Bombers May Pause", and went on to explain that they were a military novelty, that the Nazis might have prejudiced other forms of war production to concentrate on them and that they were extremely costly. Alas, much of this was wishful thinking but there is some historical interest in the report since it uses for the first time the description by which the flying bomb was initially known. It was not long however, before this same Press shortened the title to the more comfortable-sounding 'P-plane', a name which in time gave place to 'buzz bomb' from their peculiar note and finally to 'doodle bug' a name borrowed from New Zealand fighter pilots remembering the noisy insect of their own country. All of which terms were superior to the original but little-used 'robot bomber' on which Winston Churchill frowned, probably rightly, for its ring of something inexorable and against which there was no defence, smacking too strongly of the Nazi title which was '*Vergeltung 1*' – the first of the revenge weapons.

Time passed, and with it the natural resilience of people ensured that it became possible to live, however dangerously, with the missile and to adjust accordingly. The warning from the Home Secretary proved true and factories employed roof spotters from their staff who would watch for approaching bombs after the sounding of a public warning and only send workers to the shelters at the actual approach of a bomb likely to drop onto the premises. This was given in a variety of ways, a klaxon was the most common, but from others a passer-by might hear the tones of a carefully-spoken young lady announce without a trace of emotion of any kind over the loudspeaker system "Internal warning, internal warning. Take cover, take cover." The Americans did it rather better, if less attractively in the gigantic camp at Bushey when a male voice would announce in amplified metallic tones "Flying bomb, take cover! Flying bomb, take cover!"

As the weeks went by the attacks continued, often in weather more suggestive of late autumn but it was on a comparatively pleasant day, Sunday 20 June that one of the gravest incidents took place in London. It was approaching mid-morning and many worshippers were taking advantage of the fine weather to walk across St James's Park to morning service in the Guards' Chapel attached to Wellington Barracks in Birdcage Walk, where Dr Leslie Owen, Bishop of Maidstone, was to preach to a congregation of servicemen and women, civilians and relatives. This gathering which numbered some two hundred were standing following the first Lesson when a bomb was heard approaching. Expecting it to pass over, the crowd took little notice until a dreadful silence from the sky announced that the motor had cut out. At a time such as this, many had taken to counting mentally the fourteen seconds which could elapse between this and the explosion, but now thoughts were swamped by a great rushing which increased until, more swiftly than the listeners could comprehend, it culminated in an explosion which for a moment seemed to embrace all heaven and earth before the 106-year-old building collapsed about them. The destruction was complete, little more than one wall, a pair of columns and the altar remaining intact, the latter bearing the words, remarked on by many of the rescuers as they toiled to rescue the wounded and extract the dead from the piles of masonry, "Be thou faithful unto death and I will give thee a crown of life".

Many of the injuries were extremely grave, while among the 119 killed were the Commanding Officer of the Grenadier Guards, Colonel Lord Edward Hay; the Reverend Ralph Henry Whitrow, Chaplain to the Brigade of Guards; Major J. Causley Windram, their Director of Music, and Captain George Kemp-Welch of the Grenadiers, the Warwickshire county cricketer.

Less grave, rated in terms of the number of lives lost, was the occasion when there was but a single casualty, an unfortunate waitress who happened to be on the top floor when a V-1 struck the Regent Palace Hotel near Piccadilly Circus, housing some 500 guests at the time. Luckily the missile hit the annexe which was empty, although many people were in the nearby Winter Garden. But for this, the incident could so easily have been a repeat of the time during the 'blitz' when a bomb on the Café de Paris off Piccadilly Circus had claimed a hideous loss of life.

Once stimulated, the memories of those days start crowding in; newly-qualified Dr James Hardy was enjoying a quiet cup of tea with a medical friend in a small suburban tea shop, an idle glance out of the window gave him pleasure at the sight of the neatly-tended little garden round the wardens' post on the opposite corner. A girl walked by, young, slender and pretty, her legs bare, a fashion becoming increasingly popular with clothes rationing. The wind played with her skirt as she turned the corner so that James admired the line of her calves as she swung out of sight, and he thought no more about her. Minutes later the warning sounded and with its wail came the sound of a 'doodle bug'. Its motor cut out almost at once and, the adrenalin flowing, Dr Hardy and his friend flung themselves on the floor away from the window as the missile exploded up the next turning. Almost immediately it seemed, there was the sound of running feet, wardens shouting, the shrill sound of fire and ambulance bells. "Is there a doctor about?" the anguish in the cry from a rescue worker, drained it of the humour usually associated with the call. "I am." James heard himself reply. "Then for God's sake see what you can do for this poor kid!" A few minutes later the young medical man found himself trying not to vomit as, with borrowed instruments, he amputated from the same girl one of the crushed legs he had so recently admired and by which she was now pinned under a pile of masonry.

A brighter side to the destruction and suffering which the V-1s spread was that they seldom started fires although there were notable exceptions such as the call to the Aldwych which the National Fire Service received on 30 June. Firemen had prepared throughout the previous winter, however, and had established additional observation posts and trained in rescue work, so that it was common to see a fire engine making its way perhaps through back streets to avoid a diversion leading to an incident, the new route marked as likely as not by a series of notices propped against lavatory pans, an item of domestic equipment which was particularly vulnerable to the effects of bomb blast, the pedestals showing a tendency to crack.

Firemen also carried out first-aid repairs and put on emergency roofing, salvaged furniture, evacuated women and children and generally cleaned and cleared up public buildings. In addition they answered 2,380 calls between the first attack in June and the end of March the following year, the majority in June, July and August, the maximum being received on the 3 August when 97 calls were received in one day by 5 (London) Region of the N.F.S.

Not reported, like that of the Guards' Chapel, until nearly a fortnight later, were other incidents to London landmarks such as that at Carey Street where the Bankruptcy Court was demolished, damaging the near-by Law Courts, where documents were destroyed and two fire-watchers and a cleaner killed.

By this time Nazi propaganda was convincing itself and its readers that London was soon to be completely evacuated of civilians and stated: "The British Government has ordered the evacuation of London following the attacks. The population is leaving London at an unprecedented rate. It is probable that other English cities will be evacuated." In this there was certainly some germ of truth for, although the number of flying bombs reaching the coast had never attained the 2,000 per day which was now forecast by Berlin, the newspapers were openly stating that 20,000 persons had gone to safety before mid-July to such centres as Newcastle, Barnsley, Blackburn, Doncaster and Scunthorpe, the London railway stations serving those areas being crowded during a temporary lull in the attacks.

A common sight was the parked line of red, London Transport buses awaiting crowds of youngsters, all prominently identified by luggage labels on their clothing with attendant boy scouts and police ready to lend a hand with bundles and bags, to dry tears, wipe noses and calm anxious parents. Bereft of the majority of its audience and to minimize the danger brought about by large gatherings of children, the National Cinema Club, which presented films on Saturdays to juvenile audiences, was suspended.

In fact, the traffic with the north of England was a two-way one and, while children were being cared for far from London, many building workers were coming to the areas under attack to assist in the repair of buildings some of which had been damaged several times over. Robust and good-natured men, their temperament made them as likely as not replace a roof, with a prominent 'V' for Victory sign in fresh red tiles so that it stood out sharply against the faded, darker shade of the weathered material. They had need to be resilient for they were often housed in flimsy buildings about which questions began to be asked in official circles and endured the continued attacks with the same fortitude as the Londoners. Some came from further afield and many were never to see their homes again. Typical was the case of the eleven men from Scotland and Ireland who had arrived only a few hours before and were resting from the journey in huts at Croydon, Surrey erected beside a former tram depot now doing duty as a mortuary. Into this crashed a V-1 while the men were asleep and all were killed immediately.

To remedy the difficulties of accommodation, advertisements began to appear in local papers, one such running: "Wanted at once for Building Trade and other War Workers, Lodgings with breakfast, evening meals and week end meals. Usual terms: 30/- per week with allowances for extra or less meals. Apply, the Borough Valuer." The cost of £1.50 gives an interesting sidelight on the values of the day.

By now, flying bombs were becoming an accepted part of life for those in London and the Home Counties. Big Ben began to be broadcast from synchronized recordings lest any sound of an approaching V-1 should be caught by the microphone and prove of use to the enemy and the 'alert' began to be sounded now for only batches of bombs. The first hint of single missiles for residents near the defensive areas being the gunfire or the rattle of the pulse-jet, while the tendency was to sound the alarm at night and not to cancel it until daylight came again the following morning. A record of the 'alerts' was kept in a note pad among the broadcast cooking recipes which told how to make the food rations go further, by the resourceful Mrs Finch; there had been a lull in the assaults from midday until 10.30 p.m. on Friday 21 July when the siren had sounded a warning which persisted until 6.45 a.m. the following morning. Following this she recorded for Saturday: "7.15 a.m.; 7.45 a.m.; 10.20 a.m.; 11.10 a.m.; 12.10 p.m.; 1.20 p.m.; 3.15 p.m.; 4.30 p.m.; 6 p.m.; 6.35 p.m.; 9 p.m.; 10.45 p.m.", an 'alert' which continued throughout the night until the welcome sustained note of the siren at 8 a.m. the following morning when she again took up her pencil and having written "Sunday July 23rd" went on to enter: "8.20 p.m.; 2.30 a.m.; 3.15 a.m.; 4.30 a.m. ..."

The previous Saturday had seen a particularly regrettable incident near Croydon when V-1s came over just as workers were returning home at the end of the day and one struck the front of a house, part of a row. A few doors away a neighbour stood at his gate and at first thought that the bomb was coming on to his home. He rushed indoors to bundle his wife and mother under the stairs but by some caprice it turned and struck a few yards up the road. "I should think I'm one of the few people to see a flying bomb as close as that and live to tell the tale," he said afterwards. He had reason to rejoice; in the rubble of his neighbour's home, four people lay dead while rescue workers toiled to recover the bodies.

Over all the area under bombardment the strain was now beginning to tell as shown by small items of news which came to one's ears: the local amateur dramatic group was temporarily suspending its rehearsals for *Tom Jones*, one man was suing his next door neighbour for assault after allegedly receiving a punch for humorously remarking "I'll lay you six to four where that one's coming down."

The same week, Ernestine Rycroft and her younger sister, Helen, had gone to their local 'Regal' Cinema to see *The Fighting Seabees* starring John Wayne and Susan Hayward which was being screened with *Rose Marie* featuring Jeanette MacDonald and Nelson Eddy. The warning had sounded while they were enjoying the films but they decided to walk home as it was only a short distance and nothing much seemed to have happened in Purley. As they made their way along the sun-lit streets, for once the weather was kind, they were unconscious of the admiring glances which their golden-haired beauty attracted: two perfect roses scarcely in bloom. The elder and taller strode with the graceful swing given by her perfectly proportioned figure. Despite all the dreadful things that were going on life was very precious, discovering first love, poetry, music and books.

As they neared their home it seemed as if the seasons themselves were in revolt, for under their feet lay an almost autumnal carpet of leaves except that they were green, yet the air held a spring-like scent of sap. They quickened their pace as the first broken windows and doors lying at a crazy angle caught their eye; then with a shock they realized that the roof they could see caving in was that of their father's house. A group of his friends and patients had arrived and were helping to clear the mess while others had produced, as if from nowhere, a tarpaulin to cover the roof. What had happened was that a 'buzz bomb' had blown up in the garden of the house behind theirs and, with all the bangs and noise which went with the John Wayne film they had not noticed which were real and which theatrical! But cinemas could be a death-trap, performances tended to go on with only a slide to announce the sounding of the warning outside, leaving patrons to decide for themselves whether to leave or not. The wrong decision had cost several people their lives only a few miles away when they decided to remain watching Greer Garson and Ronald Coleman in *Random Harvest*.

Still there was the unwritten agreement that life should go on as normally as possible and an advertisement appeared in one newspaper in which a distinguished departmental store stated:

ROBOT PLANES

We are pleased to be in a position to announce that we have an Air Raid Shelter which can accommodate 1,500 people below our new building. Warning and the 'All Clear' are communicated to all the departments by means of a private warning system. Customers may therefore shop here with a consequent and extra sense of safety if an 'Alert' should be sounded. With the Compliments of Grant Bros. Ltd, Croydon.

The possibilities of being caught far from cover were always at the back of one's mind if one went far from home and it became the accepted practice to allow extra time for a journey by public transport. Students, perhaps condemned to a day attending lectures in their college's basement, might make an erratic journey by a tram which would stop every few hundred yards when a V-1 was heard. In this they had the advantage over buses in that the former, being comparatively quiet, allowed the driver to hear what was going on, but the petrol engine afforded no such convenience and the drivers of these and London taxis grew skilled in judging the prevailing state of affairs from observing the behaviour of pedestrians. They would stop by a public air-raid shelter if one was sufficiently handy on the route when the danger appeared too great, although this exercise in observation could present difficulties if there were not many people about, outside shopping hours.

First aid party member John Crouch remembers being called to the scene of a flying bomb incident one morning where most of the passengers from a bus had found shelter a few yards from the explosion. On the top deck he noticed several men and women who appeared to be made of sterner stuff since they were hunched in their seats seemingly waiting to be driven on. He bounded up the stairs with a cheery cry of encouragement. There was no response, yet they appeared unharmed at first glance. He approached the first and realized that he was dead as was the next and likewise the remainder. Then he realized what had happened, there was not a whole window in the bus but the passengers on top, unable to get out in time or who had not heard the conductor's call had been killed by the multiple injuries inflicted by the millions of needles of glass driven by the force of the blast and with which their bodies were now riddled.

Throughout the weeks when the misery of the weather only added to the depression caused by the showers of robots, the London Underground system offered, as it had during the blitz, shelter for an enormous number of persons. This facility was augmented in July when, on the evening of Sunday the ninth, tickets were first employed to admit those who had applied on the Saturday, not to the 'Tube' this time but to the newly-opened deep shelters at a lower level than the Underground. For the people using these the quantity of belongings to be taken down had to be regulated and was restricted to a single palliasse, no larger than 6 feet by 2 feet 6 inches, three blankets and two pillows all of which could, once brought, be left on the bunks. Shelterers, who could gain access as early as 6 p.m. but were required to leave by 8 a.m. the following morning, were advised to bring their own crockery since a canteen was also provided.

As the summer wore on the conversation in pubs and clubs, cafés, back gardens and shelters, turned mainly on two subjects; how well the Allied invasion of the Continent of Europe was going and how soon 'it' would all be over, which usually meant the war and the flying bomb attacks. But the second line of approach which every raconteur had, was the peculiar details of 'his' bomb. Usually it took the form of his remarkable escape from a seemingly hopeless situation but occasionally it could be more original and held some interest in relating just how oddly the new weapon could behave on its way to the target. One young man recalled how he used to sit outside the entrance of the garden 'Anderson' shelter and watch the 'doodles' go over through a pair of binoculars. One day his vigilance was rewarded by the sight of a missile chugging across the sky with the entire jet-unit wrapped in flames, but he was not so lucky as a neighbouring air-raid warden who counted fifteen together, one day in July. Another tale told how a single window dropped out by some freak of blast from a bomb which had passed harmlessly overhead and exploded some way off. "I beat it, old boy, just passing like I was, looked as if I'd slung a brick or something."

Another event which could have had a grim ending was that which took place on a Saturday afternoon when, hard on the wail of the siren, a V-1 hurtled down on one of a row of semi-detached homes at Waddon, west of Croydon; completely demolished, the house was empty, everyone had just left to attend the daughter's wedding.

Unfortunately, one of the best stories never came to British ears although it would have had a tremendous effect as a morale booster. It runs that at the beginning of July, Hitler was due to visit personally the area south of Cherbourg where American armoured forces had just succeeded in breaking away to the north-west and were driving onwards. The expected speech never came for the security forces were gravely worried by an unaccountable explosion which had rocked the Führer's command post. Memories of the discontent which had shown among his generals from time to time were quickly recalled and he was rushed back to Berchtesgaden under the protection of a fighter escort while investigations began as to the source of the 'outrage'. In fact all that had happened was that a V-1, its giros malfunctioning immediately after launching, had described a semi-circular course and exploded on the wrong side of the Channel! But perhaps the final smile lies in the fact that it was only about a fortnight later that a real attempt was made on the life of Hitler when a bomb, reported to have been secreted in a briefcase by Count von Stauffenberg, burst only two metres away. Perhaps the announcement in Great Britain gave some comfort to the lady in Croydon, Mrs Fitter, who, ten days later found herself sheltering under the stairs when a V-1 roared down and she had rushed out of the kitchen. "I had only just got there," she said later, "when everything seemed to collapse, I did not hear the bomb fall or an explosion." Then she found the staircase giving way and held it up with her hands until a smiling face through a hole in the rubble proved to be that of one of the rescue party. "Then I was all right."

By August, the attacks were reaching their zenith, despite the advance of British and American Armies towards the launching sites. A hope that these men would be diverted from their main objectives and therefore relieve the pressure on the Nazis was not realized but it was probably in the belief that this would happen that reports began to come through of launchings from Belgium. In London and the Home Counties a new type of 'alert' was introduced from the middle of the month in which the signal lasted for only 40 seconds instead of the former full minute and the number of upward notes was reduced from eight to five. This was an attempt to satisfy complaints that the sirens sounded for so long that people, especially those who were close to them, could not hear the sound of the first bombs arriving. This proved satisfactory and was retained but did no more than appease the now over-taut nerves of civilians who went about their duties in post office, church, flats and shops. All of these continued to suffer and had their destruction still marked by the combined smell of fine dust and of sap from the trees from which the bark as well as the leaves were constantly stripped.

Maximum delivery was reached on 2 August and three days later it was announced that the quotas for the reception areas for evacuees had been doubled. The large families had always presented a problem and these, it was announced, were now to be accommodated in former Army camps with the advantage of their communal feeding arrangements. Press reports were vague with the details, it being implied that these consisted of brick bungalows, one capable of taking 1,000

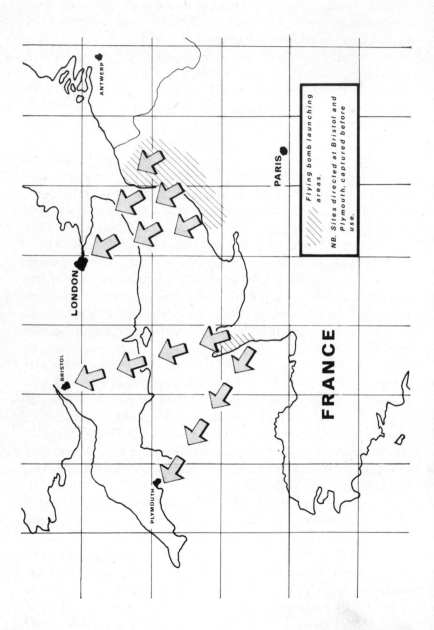

ANTWERP

PARIS

LONDON

BRISTOL

PLYMOUTH

FRANCE

Flying bomb launching areas.

NB. Sites directed at Bristol and Plymouth, captured before use.

women and children being described at Neston, near Birkenhead, but it seems that this type of thing was in fact one of the hastily-erected 'villages' intended for earlier use but never pressed into service.

The casualty figures for the month of July seemed to indicate that civilians still had to brace themselves for the continuance of the ordeal since the preceding four weeks had cost the lives of 2,441 persons, the majority, women, and 7,101 had been wounded.

At the same time as the bombardment was at its height, so too were the efforts of the propaganda machine in Berlin. This told graphic tales of the suffering in such centres as Plymouth, Portsmouth, Southampton, Weymouth, Dover, Folkestone, Gravesend, Margate and on the Isle of Wight, in all of which great fires were said to be raging from the constant rain of 'Hitler-bolts' or 'dynamite meteors' which fell on them. Certainly, the missiles continued seemingly to heave themselves over the coast, one witness remembering them crossing between Shoreham Harbour and Portslade at something like 200 feet. By now, many were being shot down into the Ashdown Forest, but in fact the damage and burning buildings were invisible to the citizens of these areas. The ordeal of Southampton was certainly grim, although it had not come from the conventionally-launched bomb, but, on 7 July from air-launched missiles, and ramps had been prepared which were aimed at Plymouth and also Bristol.

The greatest effort which the thirty-eight launching sites could show was a firing of 316 V-1s in a space of twenty-four hours, but of these, twenty-five crashed at once – an improvement on the earlier loss figure of about thirty per cent – and only something like 107 are recorded as crossing the coast. However, great efforts were being made to justify the claims of the destructive force of the bombs as described by Berlin and to this end some were fitted with a small cage designed to carry twenty-three B2-type incendiary bombs, each of 2 pounds (1 kilogramme) weight, or a paper carton filled with propaganda leaflets which, like the fire bombs, were scattered by the force of the explosion. Some of the leaflets are still preserved and it is interesting to note the photograph of German civilian slain with the caption "This is an experiment, let's try it", allegedly a remark of Winston Churchill's. There also appears an extract from a speech at Broadstairs in December 1941 by Captain Harold (now Lord) Balfour, the Conservative Member for the Isle of Thanet and Under-Secretary of State for Air. This, taken from its context as reported in *The Times* in the issue for the following Monday, makes quite different reading from the explanation, which it was, of the reasons why an officer who "abhorred the political doctrines of Communism" should visit Stalin in the line of wartime duty.

About three per cent of the V-1s launched had a small radio transmitter fitted. Under the rudder these particular machines carried a stout paper tube, the rear end of which was plugged with a circular tensioner. This, once released, drew out a length of aerial for the ranging transmitter so that a check could be maintained on the target-setting device of random missiles.

It was, of course, important that some measure of accuracy should be adopted in the aiming of flying bombs so that the concentration level might be kept up and, from time to time, reports were made of conventional machines being sighted during attacks.

But the end was in sight as British and American land forces took a stranglehold on the launching areas. This was reflected in the change of emphasis on Berlin radio. They now spoke of "nuisance raiding" or, as one British newspaper put it, "watered down the flying bombast", and despite the sombre warning that stocks of the weapon were sufficient for continued attacks for a further fortnight, according to a Swedish agency, people began to feel that the worst was over. Over, that was, as far as flying bombs were concerned and in this country, but abroad the whole sorry tale was beginning again and with the move of the launching ramps to Holland, Antwerp became the main target and suffered a total of 2,448 bombs, a number about equal to the entire British burden up to the middle of August, the majority leaving the new ramps during October. Simultaneous with these, the Belgian city was also subjected to rocket attacks with the new V-2 weapon, but in England recognition that such existed was, apart from hopeful noises from the news media, confined to speculation on the source of strange booms such as that which prompted a schoolmaster, taking prayers one morning, to remark to his boys, "Well, we could have been in a worse position".

5 | Recollection and Reckoning

The attack by flying bombs, or the "Second Battle of London" as one imaginative correspondent termed it at the time, lasted, in round figures for a period of eighty days and some tried to force the time into the same form as the Battle of Britain by dividing it into three phases, 13 June to 1 September 1944, the period of the main assault; 6 September to 14 January 1945, the air-launched period and lastly the brief 'final throw' from 3 to 29 March 1945, while during part of the later periods was the additional ordeal by V-2 rocket. However this may be, it is true that, comparatively brief as the entire series of attacks was, they created both in the minds of civilians and service men and women alike a large and rich lore which was to be remembered for many years to come.

As time went by, the pattern of life changed to cope with the frequent interruptions but the rudest shock of all came when it was realized that one could no longer depend on the cessation of the engine sound to announce imminent danger. Admittedly, this had been the case on odd occasions before but the Nazi method of solving the problem took on a sinister aspect when it was realized in the target areas that, purely for ballistic reasons, the descent on to the target was in the form of a long flat spiral with the motor still running, which explains the often-repeated tales of bombs which turned about on their tracks and seemed to take an almost human delight in fiendishly tantalizing a watcher on the ground.

Once the glee had evaporated of the first night's belief that large numbers of Nazi bombers were being set alight and falling victim to some new defence, a fresh thought took hold of the public mind crediting the 'doodle bug' with an extreme of accuracy it could not possess. There were plenty of tales to substantiate this; one had fallen on a small factory engaged in the production of airscrew blades and it was only the caprice of the wind up the river which had at the last moment diverted the missile from the actual factory buildings to the park wherein every delivery vehicle was destroyed; others disputed this and pointed out that the extreme accuracy of the weapon made it capable of picking out the lorries so that a bottle-neck of components would be created in the works and the frustrated staff, would then mutiny! An even greater nonsense was the construction put on the fact that a three-month-old baby in a house not a hundred yards away had slept through the dive and explosion and it was whispered that the new descent made no assault on the senses and one accepted the noise until it was too late. Then there was also an anecdote about an incident comparatively early in the attacks when, entirely by chance, a V-1 had demolished the London Headquarters of the Supreme Allied Commander, General Eisenhower. This event is still remembered by a member of the Royal Observer Corps because of the ease with which his uniform gained him entry and gave him an uneasy smile at the contrast between his unauthorized admission and the elaborate security checks which regularly greeted even the most high-ranking visitor. His roaming round the corridors proved of little interest, however, except for the chance to examine a length of steel tube. In fact, this was a substantial remnant from the wing spar but at the time he found himself turning over in his mind the possibility that the pipe indicated that some form of rocket motor drove the flying bomb.

With their almost personal involvement with the attacking robots, it is members of this unsung service who are still a rich source of remembrance of the later months of 1944, but their work was not entirely directed to the guardianship of civilian life, property and industry, for a section of observers was also involved in providing aircraft recognition facilities on vessels plying across the Channel in support of Operation 'Overlord', in order to minimize the danger to friendly aircraft from trigger-happy gunners. In this way, many of these observers, while facing the dangers of the sea crossing and the beach-heads, missed the dangers of the flying bombs until comparatively late and only learnt of the horrors of the new attack from their civilian friends. One such was Seaborne Observer Alex Henderson, who normally formed part of the post at Ash, off any of the main lines of attack over Kent. Having returned from Normandy, his ship, M.V. *Hapagus* was anchored in the Thames Estuary waiting for dock space in London and it was while enduring this week-long delay that he saw, for the first time, the streams of flying bombs making their way to London and the Home Counties. He was able to see at first hand the frustration of the ships' gunners, prevented from firing a shot at the robots since the chances of bringing one down on the assembled shipping was very real indeed, an unacceptable hazard in view of the shortage of vessels at that time. Then came the one seemingly intended for his ship alone. It could be heard coming for quite a long way and then it hove into sight, another dark shape with a tail of flame, flickering in sympathy with the rattled note of the motor, clearly visible even without the aid of binoculars. Then, without warning it suddenly dived to explode on the south bank with a tremendous roar, which disturbed even the card players between decks for a moment, and small particles of debris tinkled down on the deck. A matter of minutes later a river police launch came alongside.

"Any damage or casualties?" called the constable.

"No, we're OK thanks."

"Good!" and with a rising note from the engine the steersman spun the wheel and the launch swung away in a flurry of foam.

The peculiar note of the flying bomb is the memory which stays longest in the mind and a schoolboy of the period recalls an imitation of it which, at the height of the attacks, one could enjoy in miniature at a departmental store. A long glass case on a display stand contained a model of some imaginary skyline and poised above this at the right hand end of the box a small replica of a 'buzz bomb' awaited the insertion of a coin into a slot. As this dropped, the little bomb would begin a jerky journey across the roof tops, at the same time emitting a buzzing sound and flashing a torch-bulb glow from the rear of its jet unit. Having made the trip, the expected climax never came, no flash, no dive, not even a small pop to simulate an explosion, but instead a brief pause before the model shot backwards to await a further sixpence (2½p).

The same man remembers the dual rôle that the caretaker performed at his school, appearing at the sound of the 'alert' siren in his usual dust-coat, but now topped with a black steel helmet. He was as excited as the master, who, one Wednesday afternoon, leapt back into the shelter with the cry, "I say boys, I've just seen three at once!" Such was his enthusiasm that the assembled pupils, seated in serried ranks on wooden benches inside, paused with the cherries (which they had bought from a stall in the market at the top of the hill) half way to their mouths.

The school was in Croydon Surrey, the town which achieved the doubtful reputation of being the district most frequently visited by the missiles. Here, 1,400 dwellings were destroyed by 141 bombs which killed 211 people and injured 1,991 others, damaging 54,000 homes in the process, some of them several times over. The Town Clerk was among the civic visitors to a coastal gun demonstration where he saw one flying bomb actually shot in two by very accurate fire but he need not have travelled so far, for in his own borough no less than 27 of the robots had clattered to their destruction in the town during the third week of the attacks alone. Indeed, the figures for the subsequent six weeks accurately reflect the changing tide of the assault, 10, 9, 12, 19, 11 and finally 7 being plotted. But the damage was such that measures had to be taken to provide such everyday services as bath facilities, eighteen people at a time being catered for in little pre-fabricated metal cabins delivered and assembled in the street

from a converted furniture van bearing on its side the legend
'Emergency Bath Service'. The late Chief Librarian of the
town told the author of his admiration for the players and
spectators at a baseball match between Canadian and United
States soldiers none of whom even paused or 'turned a hair'
when, two days after the opening of the main bombardment, a
missile rattled across the game. This was the time when the
light blue helmets of the incident officers, largely forgotten by
the public since the days of the blitz seemed to be everywhere
to co-ordinate the emergency and rescue services. Their
operating point was marked with a small blue flag stuck
perhaps in the lower branches of a tree or on a front-garden
fence while, as likely as not, an increasing army of cats,
bewildered, frightened and hungry, scrambled over the debris
of what had once been their homes making a distressing sight
for all, but mainly for the children who remained in the target
areas.

The manner in which these, particularly the younger ones
suffered is hard to fathom; for the most part, many seemed
almost to disregard the robots completely but the effect was
cumulative and after a few weeks it was not unusual for
parents to find their little ones cowering in some corner and
trembling as they wept for no apparent reason. However these
were the little people who were capable, like five-year-old
Jennifer, of remarking during an actual attack "What a big
bang!" as a bomb exploded at the end of the street and then
calmly continuing their play. Older children could be a
problem for the Civil Defence workers since the boys and girls
who were in the streets at the time of a warning being
sounded, would congregate to gaze at the activity aloft and
more than one died in consequence. When a pub was bombed
in a suburb near to the main centre of the attack, the landlord
of the ancient coaching inn was riddled with glass which he
carried in parts of his body for the remaining twenty-six years
of his life. His neighbour, the mother of three little girls, was
dug from her ruined home shielding the youngest with her
own body, but the eldest, shocked and clinging to the hand of

a warden asked as the stretcher bearing the remains of her luckless younger sister was carried by, "Why have they covered up Elsie?"

One of the factory-roof spotters, who held the lives of all his colleagues in his hands, recalls the hours spent staring at the sky until he was ready to press the button, which would send them all to cover at the sight of a blackbird, gliding against the grey backdrop of the sky. But, true to the meticulous training as an engineer he had received, he kept a record of a grand total of 358 'alerts' and 607 flying bombs heard during his vigil on a roof in Esher. It is still preserved to this day and runs thus:

		ALERTS	MISSILES HEARD
June			
16	Friday	5	17
17	Saturday	5	18
18	Sunday	4	19
19	Monday	7	21
20	Tuesday	5	3
21	Wednesday	3	5
22	Thursday	6	47
23	Friday	9	10
24	Saturday	4	7
25	Sunday	3	1
26	Monday	2	0
27	Tuesday	11	2
28	Wednesday	13	3
29	Thursday	9	9
30	Friday	11	7
July			
1	Saturday	8	22
2	Sunday	5	15
3	Monday	6	34
4	Tuesday	6	23
5	Wednesday	3	4
6	Thursday	3	3
7	Friday	4	10
8	Saturday	2	17

		ALERTS	MISSILES HEARD
9	Sunday	3	7
10	Monday	5	3
11	Tuesday	11	3
12	Wednesday	5	14
13	Thursday	6	2
14	Friday	5	0
15	Saturday	3	0
16	Sunday	6	2
17	Monday	3	5
18	Tuesday	8	9
19	Wednesday	10	9
20	Thursday	2	12
21	Friday	12	56
22	Saturday	10	9
23	Sunday	4	4
24	Monday	7	4
25	Tuesday	2	0
26	Wednesday	3	1
27	Thursday	5	2
28	Friday	4	18
29	Saturday	4	2
30	Sunday	3	0
31	Monday	2	0

August

		ALERTS	MISSILES HEARD
1	Tuesday	1	0
2	Wednesday	4	6
3	Thursday	4	19
4	Friday	7	9
5	Saturday	3	7
6	Sunday	3	18
7	Monday	3	2
8	Tuesday	1	14
9	Wednesday	1	3
10	Thursday	3	1
11	Friday	3	0
12	Saturday	1	1
13	Sunday	1	3
14	Monday	1	3
15	Tuesday	5	2

		ALERTS	MISSILES HEARD
16	Wednesday	8	1
17	Thursday	7	1
18	Friday	1	0
19	Saturday	5	2
20	Sunday	4	17
21	Monday	4	11
22	Tuesday	2	1
23	Wednesday	3	6
24	Thursday	3	6
25	Friday	1	0
26	Saturday	0	0
27	Sunday	1	2
28	Monday	2	3
29	Tuesday	9	10
30	Wednesday	1	0
31	Thursday	7	0

As time passed, the number of flying bombs accounted for by the defences mounted, but so too did the casualties, roughly in the ratio of one per robot. The Croydon schoolboy saw his friend, Fullacre, called out of class to go to his aunt's house which had been blasted by a near miss to help clear up the mess and their mutual friend who lived in Beckenham, Kent went home one summer's afternoon and was never seen again; his parent's home had suffered a direct hit and all therein had died. Equally tragic was the case of the war worker, another of Hawker's staff who would cycle to the design office each morning from Kingston, Surrey along the river bank. The day dawned when he failed to clock on and no sign of him or his bicycle was ever seen again. His colleagues calculated that the V-1 that had landed nearby would have fallen at the exact spot where he would have been on his way to work and there was no other conclusion than that he had been blown to fragments with his machine and the unrecognizable shreds swept into the Thames and lost; a man blasted out of the world at a stroke leaving no trace behind.

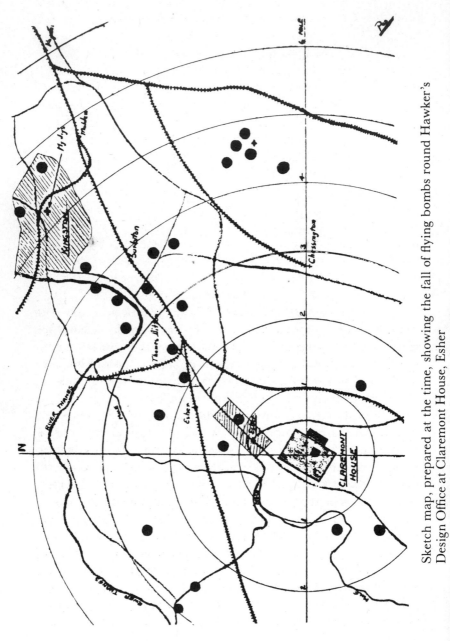

Sketch map, prepared at the time, showing the fall of flying bombs round Hawker's Design Office at Claremont House, Esher

But it was not only those in public places who died, equally one's home could be a similar death-trap. Knowing this, but half lured by fascination, there was the case of the Surrey village of Chaldon, where many people gathered outside to watch the antics of a bomb which circled their homes for several minutes, not with the long, flat spiral of the later versions but like an aeroplane waiting to land. One could hear the sighs of relief when the missile suddenly seemed to make up an almost human mind and made off in the Godstone direction, where it found a grave, harmlessly in a wood.

There was only one death at the incident when a V-1, again in Croydon, crashed on Poplar Walk, once more giving an erroneous impression of accuracy since here was the headquarters of the local Territorial Regiment. The Home Guard Headquarters too was partly destroyed, a printing works demolished and scarcely a window remained intact in the adjacent shopping centre. Housewives next day queued for their meat ration, for example, outside a shuttered butchers where a straw-hatted salesman served them from the doorway. A witness remembers the case of a robot's motor stopping at just about the same point one lunch time, causing diners and staff alike at the nearby Locarno Dining Rooms to fling themselves under the tables to take advantage of the little cover they provided.

In those days, the famous old clipper *Cutty Sark* was moored at Greenhithe, Kent and the day came when a V-1 seemed to be bent on her destruction, but at the last moment the missile turned sharply away and exploded in the River Thames. Many people during 1944 witnessed this type of thing and realized they were experiencing something new and historic. Some collected all the newspapers available (although these were in short supply and very few were on the bookstalls for casual purchase) and many carefully compiled books of cuttings. Others, as we have seen made detailed notes, scribbled down a few reactions or produced maps of the V-1s which made landfall in their particular district. A few miles up river from the old base of the *Cutty Sark* and where she now

93

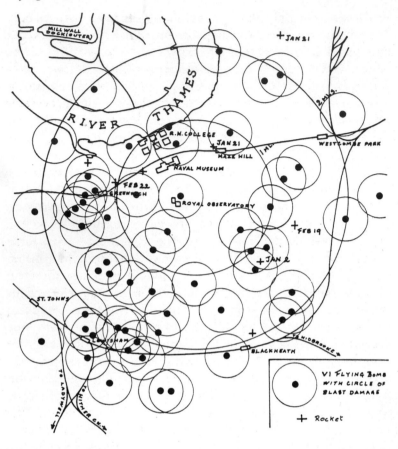

Sketch map showing the fall of flying bombs round Greenwich
Royal Observatory

rides at anchor, Mr Laurie of the Royal Observatory staff
produced a map recording the explosions round his place of
work. This gentleman was also a member of the Home Guard
and many of these volunteers gave up much time to 'parades'
not with weapons, but with tools and materials to carry out
emergency repairs on houses made uninhabitable by the latest
series of '*Vergeltung 1*' attacks. The work they did consisting in
the main of covering roofs, emergency repairs to doors and

replacing shattered glass in windows with rubberoid roofing-felt which in some areas was brought through the damaged streets by a cruising lorry or in others, could be collected by residents from a convenient local centre. Large queues could be found at perhaps a Salvation Army Citadel, members of which splendid organization were frequently among the first on the scene of an 'incident' with a mobile canteen to serve tea and snacks to victims and rescuers alike. The Y.M.C.A. provided similar help.

At this point in time, it is the small events which stay in the minds of the people who endured the attacks; the way in which carpets and floor coverings tended to be continually raised from the floor and remain until replaced in a series of bulges which gave a hollow sound when trodden on, the entry of the force of the blast through the outside air vents beneath the floor being the cause: the way in which the milkman continued to call and would often have to scramble over piles of debris from the latest bomb in order to put down the bottles. Housewives found his single appearance somewhat strange taking place as it did at about 9 a.m. each day, the pattern that all had grown up with being two deliveries, one about 6 a.m., the other near to noon. The appearance of his plodding delivery horse too was transformed in wartime by the wearing of the regulation webbing and rope halter under the normal bridle.

Under the pressure of the attacks, the reaction of the British was that of people everywhere when under strain, a sense of unification and a casting aside of the public taciturnity of peace time. For example, the Saturday afternoon when a mother and son, returning from shopping were suddenly hailed by a woman at the door of her house. A short while before the 'alert' had sounded and the couple had watched, from the cover of the doorway of a small draper's shop, a V-1 as it hurtled across the sky behind the tower of the parish church pursued by the grey and black puffs of exploding anti-aircraft shells. "Would you like to come inside and wait until this is over?" she asked, and the pair thankfully went up the

steps to take refuge in the hall. A short distance away another
flying bomb rattled over, its rhythmical note synchronized
with the spurts of red and orange flame from the jet unit,
shooting back for about the length of the fuselage. In a few
minutes a cashier at a butchers was to hear its ominous
approach and making a rush for safety in the large
refrigerator, returned after the explosion to find the desk
where she worked covered in splinters of glass.

These were the sorts of thing which became everyday topics
of conversation. One evening three men in the Strand had
dived for cover at the approach of the familiar sound. One had
reacted less swiftly than his fellows and when the dust cleared
he was nowhere to be seen. In the immediate surrounding
area of London, some people never had any freedom from the
bombs and would daily commute from one danger where they
lived to that where they worked. One such was the girl whom
an elderly female clerk carried along the corridors of Lambeth
Town Hall unmindful that her charge's severed leg was
leaving a trail of blood staining the immaculate floor. But
despite an atmosphere such as this, the general air was one of
cheerfulness as witness the lady cleaner who arrived at the
ruins of the office block where she was due to work, only to
observe to those standing by "Never pays to be too early,
mate!" on learning that a bomb had landed only some short
while before. She might have been less humorous had she
realized that the rescue parties, their helmets with a large 'R'
in front and behind, marking them out from the other boiler-
suited squads, were toiling to prise out the corpses of the Fire
Guards who had been on watch all night, only to die with the
dawn.

At the same time, there was, as there must be among a
people who watch an unending programme of suffering and
violence, a hardening of the natural humanities, at least on the
surface. A Press reporter found a rent book in the gutter where
its red covers attracted his attention. Picking it up he took it to
a civil defence worker. "She's dead," said the warden with a
glance at the name and straight away flung it back into the

pile of debris. On the other side of the coin, there was a spirit of defiance abroad as the dawn of peace seemed almost at hand, and it was not unusual to see a Union Jack fluttering above some fresh ruin. Tales were told of trapped victims, particularly among the young people, who uninjured but impossible to extract immediately, elected to remain entombed for upwards of several days accepting food, water and medical care on the end of a rope, so that the toiling gangs above could divert their attentions to others at hand whose need seemed greater.

Apart from the loss of life there were, too, other losses which time could never replace, an historic building, an ancient monument, a much loved painting perhaps. At Banstead in Surrey, an ancient forge had stood for several hundreds of years, its blacksmith attending to the needs of the farming community it once was. The life with which it was associated was a leisurely one centred about the church that manifested the simple faith of a bygone age. One wonders what the thoughts of its skilled but easy-going people would have been, could they have known that what to them would certainly seem to be a bat from hell, itself born of a world gone insane, would one summer's day rend the sky and, with the swift destruction of an avenging Lucifer, tear apart the centre of the blacksmith's craft and obliterate it for ever into the dust from which it had come.

Elsewhere there had stood for many generations an ancient gateway. It had weathered many a storm, been opened to admit children to baptism, men with fresh young brides on their arms and finally borne aloft on the shoulders of their fellows. It had been the destruction of the church by accidental fire, the change of the area from agricultural husbandry to subtopia and suffered depredations by Cromwell's troopers who called it "Popish". Then, in the summer of 1944, a flying bomb had landed close at hand demolishing a mission hall in doing so. The old gate had stood but a new set of scars now defaced its stonework, a few more flakes were gone from its coping and cornices and the expressions on the faces of its stone angels, each thrusting out a shield across her breast, became a little more obscure.

As with all events, great and small, the people who arrived at the site of a V-1 incident were often no more than onlookers, who gathered in the hope of seeing something sensational and to estimate, and exaggerate, the imagined numbers of dead from curtained and unattended ambulances driving away "How many do they get in one of those?" "They must all be finished, poor souls, there's nobody with them." Many of these spectators would keep their eyes open for souvenirs which could be carried away. Frequently this was no more than a small jagged fragment and did little harm but on the removal of anything larger and recognizable, the attendant police were apt to frown and discourage. For from hundreds of such sites there were accumulated, by the Ministry of Aircraft Production, components, large and small, that were sorted and identified until a complete, if heavily damaged flying bomb and its engine could be built up and its workings and secrets studied. At a slightly later date, exactly the same thing was done to probe the details of the V-2. The resultant composites, although mainly assembled for the use of those in charge of counter-measures and Intelligence, were shown at Farnborough's R.A.E. to the Press who, with an eye to the prevailing climate of public opinion, made much of the fact that the work was being done by "young scientists", some reporters added "brilliant", working under the supervision of "older, more experienced technicians". The manner in which this type of massive jigsaw assembly could have surprising results is told a little later, for it was to father a whole range of offensive 'ironmongery' with which we are bedevilled today.

Presentation of cold figures is the tool of dishonest statesmen and does no more than blind a reader, but it may be some indication of the size and depth of the problem set by these new assaults by unconventional weapons if, from an average bombarded district, the fourth in Greater London, Camberwell, the following figures are quoted and their related equivalent realized in terms of human suffering, and bravery.

Killed and injured: 924; homes damaged beyond repair or destroyed: 1,182; damaged but repairable in time: 7,365, requiring a labour force of 2,014 to right them. Small wonder that before the attacks finally dwindled away, 4,195 applications were received for re-housing, but perhaps the final victim of the V-1 was the Frenchman, George Claud, who, in a Europe eagerly seeking scapegoats, was arrested for allegedly "inventing the flying bomb and selling it to the Nazis". The cry of "collaborator" which was loud in the land at this time was not always justified and there is little doubt that he was innocent.

6 | 'Crossbow'

As the Allied Armies advanced into Europe it became obvious that the range of the V-1 was insufficient to cope with the greater distance from which they had to be launched and as a result, this was extended by the simple expedient of enlarging the fuel tank. Examination of the surviving specimens of altered missiles today reveals that to achieve this, an additional section of the tubular fuselage was welded on the fore part of the original and the length of the war-head, now wood-faired, and accordingly its capacity, were proportionately reduced. These were first launched on 3 March 1945 from Delft in Holland.

It was obvious then, that the Nazis were determined to continue the attacks, but even before this, the British defences were prepared for a lengthy bombardment, to counter which a policy of flexible strategy was adopted.

When the initial launchings were made on 13 June, the London Defence Area was laid out roughly in the form of a triangle with the capital as its apex and one side along the southern bank of the Thames Estuary so that the base ran approximately between Dover and Hastings. Across the middle of this was flung a wide band defended by anti-aircraft guns behind which lay the balloon barrage, while the other side, extending to the coast and out over the Channel the sky was patrolled by fighter aircraft under the guidance of G.C.I. (Ground Controlled Interception) radar stations.

Although this system looked very well on paper, practical experience showed that maximum advantage could be taken of none of the defences as they were operating then, with the result that more bombs were penetrating than there should

100

have been. One of the problems which contributed to this state of affairs was that there was little co-ordination of the intercepting fighters so that they tended to concentrate in confused groups in certain parts of the sky whenever flying bombs appeared, leaving others to go on their way without hindrance. To add to the confusion, free-ranging fighters, both RAF and American would enter the area to take part, some of them quite unsuited by their performance for overtaking a target capable of a speed in the region of 400 m.p.h.

The gunners too, had their problems, despite the fact that the missiles fulfilled all the requirements of a seemingly ideal target which flew at a constant speed and height and was incapable of evasive action. In fact the 'doodle bug' was not at all an easy target, the majority came across at an altitude of between 2,000 and 3,000 feet, where the guns were least effective because it was above the range of the light weapons and below that of the larger. This was also a height band which was low for accurate prediction by radar.

An additional problem was that of the 952 guns deployed in the London Defence Area a fortnight after the attacks opened, a high proportion were of the 3.7 inch variety. This was an excellent weapon which had been introduced in January 1938 and had quickly earned a reputation for reliability. Fitted with power rammers and automatic fuse setters, it weighed 20,541 pounds, was capable of employment on either a static or mobile mounting and had a loose liner with 156.985 inches of rifling. Coupled with an elevation range between minus five degrees and eighty degrees, it could fling a 29-pound high-explosive shell to a ceiling of 32,000 feet – all the requirements of a modern weapon, but it suffered from one serious drawback for the type of work now being asked of it, an inability to be smoothly traversed at high speed so that it could not equal the performance of the power-controlled static guns. A vital decision was taken therefore to exchange all these guns with those of the power-controlled type.

In addition to the guns of Anti-Aircraft Command in the

101

London area, there were 560 light weapons, manned by the RAF Regiment on the south coast and their successes added to the 'bag' achieved by their Army colleagues made a grand total of 309 bombs destroyed during the month after they first crossed the coast. At first this figure seems impressive but it must be viewed in the light that a proportion of the total had probably not been shot down at all but had terminated their flight as prearranged by the Nazis. Moreover the figure becomes considerably less dramatic when it is compared with that claimed by the fighters which was 883.

From this it is evident that the fighters had solved their problems thanks to the suggestions of Wing Commander R.P. Beamont DSO DFC who flew to Number 11 Group Headquarters to place before his seniors the following solutions.

Most important of these was the proposed restrictions of interceptors to three types alone, namely the Hawker Tempest 5, which was just entering service, the Spitfire and those models of the North American Mustang that had boosted motors, which would give them an even chance of overhauling the 'chuff bomb' as it was named by a minority in the RAF.

Secondly, he suggested that the problem of actually spotting one of the missiles be obviated by the firing of rockets from Royal Observer Corps posts in the direction of any missiles which they observed, to attract the attention of pilots who had been positioned by G.C.I. in the vicinity of a bomb but who still had to pick out the small, dark, high speed target against the pattern of the terrain below.

When these measures were adopted, in the remarkably short period of four days, it was found that the number of 'kills' rose in consequence, the R.O.C. contribution being made by firing 'Snowflake' illuminating rocket flares which would be easily seen from the air, the measure being known as Operation 'Totter'.

Yet, despite these aids, the V-1 was never an easy quarry, although it had the advantage of being incapable of taking evasive action. The difficulties were played down to the general public, for the Press got hold of such letters as one which had been privately sent by a pilot to his family, obviously with an eye to making his own contribution to the maintenance of morale. He wrote, "I had looked upon these doodle-bugs as toys, RAF aircrews for the amusement of, because, oh boy! they do give us lots of fun". Other newspaper reports took the same line and such headings as "Potting at Flying Bombs, New Sport" and "A Good Target", gave prominence to reassuring utterances on the lines of "The robot plane makes quite a good target although the flame from the rocket [*sic*] does make aiming difficult at times".

The tactics, which experience dictated, took the form of approaching the bomb at a greater height and then diving on it to pull out and bring the guns to bear at about three hundred yards range. At first, there was some natural reluctance to approach too close since no one knew what would happen to the fighter unable to take evasive action in time, but the day came when a Tempest pilot found he had no alternative but to carry on through the blast and he and everyone else was surprised to find that the machine was only a little the worse for wear. Admittedly, it was discovered only later that this type of machine which, by the end of the 'battle', was to be responsible for the destruction of 636 robots, had a tendency to have the fabric of the tail controls set alight when passing through the effects of just under 2,000 pounds of 'Amatol' explosive being detonated, but this difficulty was met by the development by Hawkers of a fireproof 'paint' for the final finish.

At first, an average of 500 rounds of ammunition had to be fired before a flying bomb would explode, perhaps because the early attacks were most frequently delivered from the rear with the result that the cannon shells tended to bounce off the cylindrical surface without causing damage, coupled with the early difficulties encountered in estimating range. However about eight weeks later the average number of rounds expended had been dramatically reduced to only 150 before a missile was blown up.

103

An eyewitness describes how he saw a Spitfire from 322 Squadron approach a pair of missiles, one at a slightly greater altitude than the other. Diving on the higher one, it required no more than a three second burst to explode it before a sharp bank to port brought the fighter above and to one side of the second robot which was similarly despatched.

But gun fire was not the only means of bringing down the bombs. A new method was rapidly discovered, whereby if a fighter dived past a 'doodle', the resulting turbulence from the propeller would upset the course of the bomb sufficiently for it to be caused to dive, often on its back and out of control by the gyros, to explode harmlessly in open country or the sea.

A second method of destruction by unorthodox means was discovered by a Flying Officer of 616 Squadron, 'Dixie' Dean, operating the new and untried Gloster Meteor jet fighter. Attacking a V-1, at 1,000 feet near Tonbridge, the cannon jammed and so the squadron's first victory over the new weapon was achieved when Dean flew alongside and tipped it over with his wingtip so that it crashed.

This method was soon copied by pilots of conventional fighters and one of the first received great publicity in the newspapers. This was twenty-three-year-old Flying Officer Kenneth Collier, formerly a meat inspector from Glebe, Sydney. Spotting a flying bomb which had been damaged by three fighters and was now in a shallow dive, Collier manoeuvred his machine up to the missile and, so the report ran, using his wingtip "like a spoon" threw the robot off course for several thousand feet so that the houses towards which it at first appeared to be heading escaped and the bomb crashed into the garden of an old people's home where it only blew in the windows and caused some cases of shock.

During this time, many areas gained a reputation for being absolute magnets for bombs and it is certainly true that several fell over a period of time on the same spot. One such, near the much-punished Surrey town of Croydon, was the St Helier area of Carshalton and it is true that the district immediately south of this received about a quarter of all the V-

1s which crashed on neighbouring Sutton and Cheam. It was about midday when a bomb appeared to be making its way in this direction that a watcher heard another sound above the staccato rattle of the bomb: "Simultaneously, coming over my head and converging on the 'doodle' was one of our 'Spits', neither seemed to be all that high. Now the fighter seemed to reach the bomb and ride along beside it but a trifle lower, then suddenly rising and using his right wing the Spitfire must have nudged or jolted the bomb in such a manner that it turned at right angles, dropped several feet as it did so and went out of my sight towards our little park."

The Gloster Meteor fighters of 616 Squadron had drawn their first 'blood' on 4 August, as already told, when 'Dixie' Dean stumbled across the ease with which the V-1 could be thrown out of control even at 360 m.p.h. A little under half an hour later, Flying Officer Rogers had shot down another and a further eleven were claimed by the end of the month.

These operations are of historical interest in that these were the first jets to be used on work for which they seemed ideal due to their superior performance. By this time the squadron was operating from Manston in Kent and had only eight of the new machines on strength at the time to replace the Spitfires which they had previously flown. The new arrivals had begun to appear at Culmhead, the first being delivered in July and it was immediately recognized that no time should be lost in gaining experience of their use against the V-1 despite the fact that the new fighter was still in the development stage and trials had still to be carried out by AFDU. Consequently it was decided to detach a single Flight ahead of the main squadron to Manston where four of the eight on strength could be used "if a suitable opportunity arises".

The endurance of these early jets was limited to only fifty minutes and so the maintenance of continuous standing patrols was not possible although, with experience this time was doubled, but with a rate of climb of 3,300 feet per minute and a maximum speed of 410 m.p.h., albeit at a greater height than the operational ceiling of the bombs, this was no great problem when operations were begun on 10 July.

In addition, a pair of machines was detached at Culmhead in order that all pilots could become familiar with the new type as soon as possible and great precautions were taken to preserve secrecy, Meteors being forbidden to fly closer than fifteen miles to the enemy-occupied coast.

That something new was being pressed into service against the missiles was, however, no secret to the civilians living in what the reporters of 1944 christened "fly-bomb alley" and they soon described the strange noises from the sky as, "with a noise like an express train whistling through a tunnel" jet fighter pitched into jet bomb and the cry would go up that "The 'jetties' are coming" as people gathered outside their homes to gaze at the new spectacle.

Frequently they would see nothing but heavy grey clouds with a thunder-like roar above them to bear witness that something was going on. The summer that year was one of the poorest many could recall and it is obvious that this had a serious effect on the efficiency of the defences. During the early measures against the V-1 when the intercepting fighters had full freedom of action over all that part of south-east England in front of the guns and out over part of the Channel and if the weather was sufficiently clear the codeword 'Flabby' was passed and the guns held their fire to give the fighters priority.

Medium weather was denoted by the codeword 'Fickle' and under these conditions fighters were permitted to chase bombs over the gun area up to the balloon line and observers with the batteries on the ground ensured that fire was withheld, while under bad climatic conditions the word 'Spouse' was passed to indicate that full freedom of action was to be enjoyed by the gunners up to 8,000 feet and fighters were expected to keep clear.

Fighter patrols extending over the sea could, on occasion give rise to amusing incidents one of the best being the tale of the fighter pilot who was feeling pleased with himself towards the end of his patrol at having destroyed no less than three missiles. The first had been sent spinning down by the wash of his slipstream, the second had fallen to his guns, and another, he had turned over with his wingtip. But the most unusual was that which he attempted to deal with similarly to the first, in the event not quite so successfully for the bomb on this occasion refused to be sent down by the dive of the fighter past it but only suffered a diversion from its set course and continued its way back towards France! This was not unusual, the majority falling into the sea before crossing the occupied shore. However this one continued relentlessly on and finally fell not to the British defences but to the crew of a Nazi gun battery which obligingly shot it down near Boulogne!

Throughout the attacks by flying bombs there infrequently appeared manned Nazi aircraft. On the night of the opening of the assault both a Junkers 88 and a Messerschmitt had been shot down, the latter by a Mosquito, and daylight launched bombs continued to come across under observation from the crews of the new Messerschmitt 410 twin-engined fighter. The purpose of these was obviously to monitor the accuracy of the V-1 which had to have its course predetermined and set 'blind' and it has been only recently revealed that agents in this country deliberately fed back to the Nazis information which would mislead them into believing that the course settings which had in fact caused a cluster of the weapons to fall on central London were bombarding an area to the north of the intended vicinity so that the resultant 'correction' would actually cause future missiles to fall short of the intended target.

The strain of the unceasing patrols which were called for to combat the V-1 was considerable, a publication in the United States told how fighter pilots began work at 3 a.m. and frequently had to continue until after dusk. Intercepting bombs launched after dark did have the advantage that the flame from the jet-motor could be picked out at some distance and it is recorded that the earliest of these were to cause some bewilderment to Allied pilots on their way to support the invasion of the Continent as they saw below, strange lights pursuing an unchanging, straight course below them. Of the several types used to intercept V-1s at night, the Mosquito was undoubtedly the most successful, accounting as it did for 486; American-crewed P-61 Black Widow fighters, the first United States machine to be specifically designed for night interception, were also used with success in company with the RAF's Hawker Tempest which was now enlarging its score achieved on daylight patrols, after the fall of darkness. A pilot of one such who endured considerable publicity somewhat later was twenty-four-year-old Squadron Leader Joseph Berry, DFC and Bar, who on one patrol during the hours of darkness accounted for seven robots and emerged at the end of the attacks with a total of sixty having fallen to his guns.

Wing Commander Roland Beamont, DSO and Bar, DFC and Bar, has already been mentioned at the beginning of this chapter, and it is he who is credited with the perfection of the ideal method of attacking the missiles from above and astern. This was the result of the practice of discussing, each evening outside the cottage which served as a Wing Intelligence Office, methods of approach and attack to be tried out next day. During this period his responsibilities were heavy in the extreme, not only calling for duties of this sort but also participation in actual patrols, from dawn to dusk during which he amassed a personal 'score' of twenty-seven.

Although the work of the fighter pilots was of course the spearhead of anti-'Diver' measures, behind this was a system of control and raid reporting more complex than any which had been devised to date. Two methods of control were used; the first of these was known as 'Running Commentary' and was chiefly utilized for the control of fighters over land. For this two radar stations and two R.O.C. centres were used, at each of which was a controller whose duty it was to transmit to pilots the course and position of flying bombs, rather than give exact courses to be followed, and leave the individual pilot to intercept in his own way. This system did suffer from the disadvantage that no separate vectors or courses were transmitted with the result that some wastage of effort could result if more than one pilot should pursue a single bomb. But, broadly speaking, it worked well, particularly when used in conjunction with the R.O.C. rocket signals, Wireless Observer Units or marker gunfire by day, while at night, searchlights marked the passage of bombs for the interceptors as well as giving warning of the proximity of barrage balloons, which could be alternatively indicated by the 'Snowflake' rockets.

The other system of fighter control was known as the 'Close Control' method and was employed for fighters over the Channel. It called for the location of controllers at each of three coastal radar stations thus enabling them to make use of the data on approaching V-1s immediately it became available. With this information controllers could direct fighters to meet individual bombs by means of radio.

The drawback to this system was that the bombs were over the sea for only a short period of time, particularly in the region of the narrow Dover Straits and the range of the radar coverage was limited so that interception was difficult in the period of perhaps four or five minutes during which a missile was over the sea. Coupled with this was the fact that the vicinity was constantly busy with friendly aircraft involved in the Allied invasion programme, particularly when British and American air forces were supporting the battle on the ground as it swung out of the Normandy area, with the result that radar operators found it difficult to distinguish the 'blips' of flying bombs on their screens from those of the friendly armada. Despite these problems, the system was continued due to the desirability of bringing down as many 'doodle bugs' over the sea as possible.

So far only the work which dealt with Royal Observer Corps co-operation with the fighters has been recounted, but the responsibility of this service went far beyond that. The system of initiating the plotted course of a bomb began with a radar-detected report from the RAF filter room. At first there would be no confirmation that the plot was that of a V-1 but this would be quickly indicated by the constant course and speed observed. Once this was established the information was prefixed to the plotter on the Long Range Board at an R.O.C. centre by the priority warning 'Diver-Diver-Diver' which was repeated by the Sea Plotter as he snapped in place the magnetic plastic arrow and placed alongside a black, blue and red plaque giving the raid number, prefaced with an oversized red disc, plus the speed and height. Alerted by the codeword, the plotters on the main table then warned their post clusters of the possible presence of a 'diver', possible, because there was still time during which it might be brought down by the defences, or even, rarely turn out to sea again. While this was going on, the Duty Controller might exhibit on the front of his dais, high above the plotters and commanding a view of the entire operations room, a warning sign that 'Diver' was in operation, an immediate reminder to any observers coming on duty.

As the attack developed, any plaques belonging to missiles destroyed *en route* would be removed from the sea plotter's position by a raid orderly and the crew would brace themselves for the appearance of bombs over their Group area.

Once it was established that there was a serious danger, the air-raid warning officer from Home Security, who occupied a place among the R.O.C. officers on the dais, would warn the most likely districts to be effected by the missiles and from this the public 'alert' sirens were sounded.

Meanwhile, outside, in fields, high on the vantage points afforded by public buildings and in open spaces, perhaps some of the posts, alerted by the centre would detect the characteristic rattle of a bomb's motor and call up the operations room with exact information on the direction of the note and data from which the plotter could calculate the possible height. While doing this, they would place on the ring marking the post's periphery on the main table, a small plastic 'sound trumpet', so named from its shape and by taking cross bearings on this plot and reports from adjacent posts it would be immediately possible to mark the position of the bomb.

This might be followed by others in succession or reports of a visually-established track which would be marked not by the shield-shaped counters of the sound track but by arrows with, alongside, narrow plaques giving data on the identification number and altitude which tellers on the dais would be passing to adjacent centres in case the missile passed on to one of the neighbouring areas. Then, quite suddenly, an observer at an outside post would hear the noise of the motor suddenly stop, immediately he gave his call-sign over the field telephone and add "Diver cut!" almost at the same moment, an experienced plotter at the main table would shout the information across the operations room, adding the identification number, "Diver 242 cut!" and the cry would be repeated to the warning officer with the added grid reference which would give the vicinity in which immediate alarm had to be given to factory workers who would have ignored the public 'alert', "Diver 242 cut, Queenie 2473!" the table supervisor would shout and at the same moment the plotter put a crash counter beside the last reported position of the missile. Somewhere, outside, there would be a boom and a rumble and a column of smoke would climb lazily into the sky. The A.R.W.O. would glance down at the table and if there were no further robots likely to descend on the immediate area, throw the switches which would release the factory workers to resume their tasks. Meanwhile, once the other 'Divers' on the main table had been accounted for, attention would swing back to the Sea Plotter at the edge of the vertical Long Range Board where the excitement began and if no further bombs were appearing as 'blips' on the RAF's radar screens to be fed in to the R.O.C. operations room, the same voice which had started it all might release the tension by calling the welcome announcement, for the moment at least, "Diver cancelled".

As on other branches of the defence organization of these islands, the pressures brought about by this type of work were enormous, not only in the centre operations rooms but, of a different kind, on the posts as well, where more than one

111

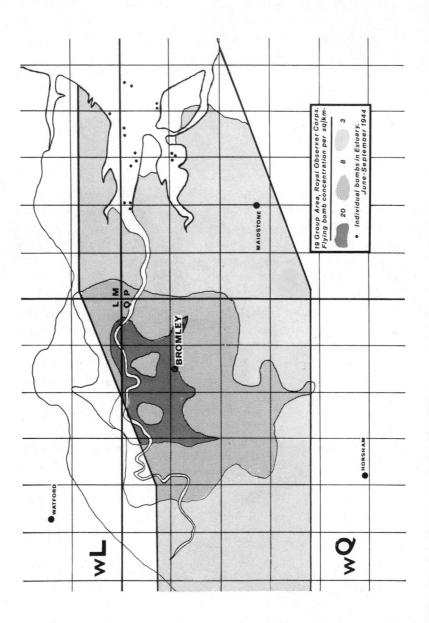

19 Group Area, Royal Observer Corps.
Flying bomb concentration per sq/km.

20   8   3

● Individual bombs in Estuary.
June–September 1944

WATFORD ●

MAIDSTONE ●

● HORSHAM

L M
O P

● BROMLEY

wL

wQ

112

observer was killed while on duty against flying bombs. It was decided therefore to introduce into the centres guarding the Home Counties, additional personnel, almost entirely female, to relieve the regular crews. Many of these girls came from those areas where the work had been for some time light and in which the V-1 was, as yet, something which was only reported in the newspapers and on radio in the security-conscious phraseology that "Flying bombs were launched against Southern England". It was a party of young women such as this that an officer was detailed to meet on arrival to augment the hard-pressed crews of the Bromley, Kent Centre and his first duty was to conduct them to their billets in order that they might rest after the rigours of the rail journey. It was only a matter of a few hours later that this same officer was among the first on the scene with pick and shovel to assist in releasing the entombed girls from the wreckage of their temporary home which had collapsed when the first 'doodle bug' they had ever heard cut its motor at just the wrong place and destroyed with a direct hit the houses only a few yards away.

Royal recognition of the vital work which the R.O.C. was expected to perform during the assault came early in the bombardment when Post E. (Easy) 4 of Number 17, Watford Group was visited on 18 June 1944, the Sunday following the opening of the attacks, by their Majesties King George VI and Queen Elizabeth (now the Queen Mother) in company with Princess Elizabeth (our present Queen) and the Hon. Andrew Elphinstone. Observers on duty in the Windsor Castle Post at the time were D. Southeard and F.R. Hazell and five 'P-planes' as they were still being called in the Press, had crashed in the area commanded by the watchers on the Brunswick Tower, one of them into Staines New Reservoir, at about the time of the visit which was near to 11 p.m.

In the minds of the general public, the heroes of the hour were the fighter pilots of the RAF and letters extolling their skill such as that to the *News Chronicle* telling of a damaged flying bomb, its engine stopped, being supported by the wing of a fighter aircraft until it was clear of a built-up area, were typical of public feeling. Admittedly, the civilian was very conscious of the RAF's balloon barrage which extended from Cobham to Limpsfield, a wall of some 2,000 balloons, but they lacked drama and the feelings of the public were mixed. Although they were instrumental in bringing down some bombs. Some had been fitted with one type or another of cable cutter, but occasionally things could go awry and at least one case is known in which the cutter fouled the cable instead of severing it and the bomb was brought down prematurely on several houses (at Wallington in Surrey) by the drag of the additional load.

The arrangement of the capital's defences at the beginning of the flying-bomb attacks

As for the guns, after their first showing they seemed to have lost the public's interest. This frame of mind of the civil population was grossly unfair. The number of robots which they had destroyed to date was certainly unsatisfactory to everyone, most of all to the gunners, but, sandwiched between the area allocated to the fighters, to which they were obliged to give precedence as has been explained, and the narrow band of balloons at their back, they had little chance to show their mettle.

Just before the middle of July it was decided to remedy this and give the gunners an uninterrupted field of fire by what Mr Duncan Sandys was later to describe with magnificent understatement as a "bold step". This was nothing less than a project to move the entire anti-aircraft gun area to the coast. The decision was taken at a time when some redeployment had only just been completed, brought about by the replacement of the 3.7 inch guns. This alone had called for a mighty effort involving as it did the invention of a prefabricated mounting for the new, power-operated weapons, since the laying of concrete foundations was out of the question in the time available. These guns had to be brought from outlying areas and replaced there by hand-operated guns, the lighter ones moved forward and with them the entire complex of stores, fire-control, communication and telephone lines, often to sites without power or water, and the establishment of a dozen new communications rooms. Indeed, either by road or rail, some of the anti-aircraft defences had endured a double move brought about by the deepening of the balloon belt, so it will be seen that this anticipated re-deployment was undertaken in full knowledge of the magnitude of the task.

Credit for the new concept must go to Air Commodore Ambler, deputy Senior Air Staff Officer to the C-in-C, Fighter Command, Air Marshall Hill (later Sir Roderick Hill) and Robert (later Sir Robert) Watson-Watt, who had 'fathered' radar in Great Britain. The Air Marshal immediately agreed to the new idea but expressed some doubts as to the acceptance by the Anti-Aircraft C-in-C, General Sir Frederick Pile who, not knowing that the Fighter Command chief had already been approached, expressed his own doubts about acceptance by the RAF! In the event both men realized that they had in some measure misjudged each other in

115

erroneously believing that either would put the potential for his own Service before the demands of national defence and the mammoth undertaking was agreed on, although not without serious misgivings by the Air Council.

Quite apart from the obvious advantages to be gained from a greatly widened operating area, another lay in the fact that the guns were now operating with new radar sets of the SCR 584 GL type which, employed near to the coast, would be able to give readings without interference by the ground contours to be found inland, while, additionally, the new Variable Time Fuse could be fitted without the danger to civilians which it presented when used over a built-up district.

The plan was submitted on 13 July and although some of the heavy guns were moved the following day, the bulk shifted within the following twenty-four hours, so that the first of the large weapons was back in use again by the seventeenth, while the light guns, left in position to cover the move of the heavies were shifted afterwards and back in use two days later.

The resultant new layout was a belt of guns commanding the sea from St Margaret's Bay, Dover to Beachy Head, 15,000 yards deep extending for one third that distance inland and two thirds over the sea.

But this was not all. There had been for some time indications that some of the flying bombs were being launched on such a course that they travelled up the Thames Estuary. This was already defended by Naval and Maunsell Forts, actually sited considerable distances off shore. Their original use had been to prevent the penetration of mine-laying aircraft over the previous period of about two years, but now they were in the nature of advanced posts against bombs launched on the alternative course by virtue of their ability to give warning of the approach of missiles some ten to thirteen miles ahead of other stations. With the naval forts, seven in number, they consisted of a series of girder-supported towers, often about seven connected by a series of catwalks equipped with anti-aircraft guns and radar and manned by between 80 and 120 officers and men. To augment this line of defence by the

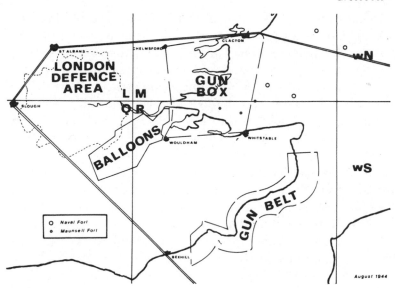

The London Defence Area, modified in the light of experience, in August 1944

Artillery, plans were drawn up to enlarge these by a series of sunken barges. At the same time they were to be reinforced by a Gun Box, north and south of the river in an area bounded by Clacton and Chelmsford on one side and Wouldham and Whitstable on the other. This was to be armed with a total of 658 guns, 208 of them of heavy calibre and the remainder a mixture of 40 mm and 20 mm weapons.

The American contribution to this was at first 165 SCR 584 gun radar sets as has already been mentioned, but, in addition it was not long before twenty anti-aircraft batteries from the same source joined the defences using their 90 mm guns.

But, good as the centimetric-wavelength radar was, a considerable improvement in the number of V-1s now accounted for by the guns was due to the proximity fuses introduced for the shells. The heart of these was a miniature valve small enough to be included in the narrow confines of a fuse and yet sufficiently strong to take the shock of the actual firing. The delicacy of these fuses may be judged by the fact

that they had been known to explode when within about 50
feet (15 metres) of a heavy cloud! This excellent device may be
termed an Anglo-American one for, although it is true that the
development was carried out across the Atlantic, it consisted
of little more than an application of the principles developed
by Pye Radio and E.M.I. in this country.

Figures available after the first week of the new deployment
showed that the guns were now accounting for some 20 per
cent of all the bombs launched and making landfall in this
country, a figure which had been more than doubled only one
month later, facts which immediately became apparent to
everyone and the tone of the reporting media changed, at first
cautiously announcing "New gun defences in action against
robots," finally culminating in such headlines as "A.A get
more flying bombs", following the day when, of the 96 V-1s to
cross the coast, 68 fell to the gunners.

So swiftly had events moved, that it is not until the end of
August was approaching that we find a concerted attempt
being made to regularize the co-ordination of balloons,
aircraft and guns. Perhaps the most far-reaching change had
been that brought about for the interceptors which now
ranged freely in the wide area between the Gun Belt and the
balloons, forward of the eastern limits of the Gun Box and
over the Channel beyond the boundary of the Gun Belt.
Outside these limits the fighters were obliged to fly at a
minimum altitude of 10,000 feet, the guns for their part being
prohibited from engaging any aircraft higher than 8,000 feet.
Hazards to fighters continued to be marked as before by
searchlights by night and the red glow of 'Snowflake' flares,
but during the hours of darkness, the seaward limits of the
Gun Belt were indicated by means of illuminated marker
buoys, the laying out of which was not finally completed until
29 August.

The same instruction which set out these measures also
embraced the rules for ships at sea since the Channel was now
busy with armed vessels of many types, plying in support of
Operation 'Overlord'. Gunners at sea were prohibited from

engaging a flying bomb if a friendly fighter was within two miles and in conditions of visibility of under three, and then only when the missile was clearly recognized and during daylight. Naturally, at this time the remarks about the traffic in the Channel sea lanes applied equally to the air when thousands of aircraft movements, unconnected with 'Diver' defence made the problems of ensuring their safety more acute so that the narrow bands of sky designated from time to time had to cope with all friendly aerial traffic.

A curious event took place on 28 August when a large party of civic visitors which included mayors, air-raid precaution controllers and town clerks, was invited to see the type of work which the guns were doing on the coast. As so often happens, the activity which had marked the beginning of the day had faded and by the time they arrived, there was little to excite them. However, it was not long before a fresh batch of V-1s showed up on the radar screens and the guns opened fire in spectacular fashion. The effect on the party was electric, the few notes as to the prowess of the ground defences which had been put out by radio and in the newspapers had seemingly gone unnoticed in favour of such announcements that the Owls' Aviary, the Hippo House, the Pheasantries and the small refreshment counter at the London Zoo would have to be rebuilt after robot damage, and the dignitaries who now witnessed the standard of the British shooting found it difficult to believe their eyes. Indeed, so impressed were they that a spokesman asked permission to pass on what he had seen so that one and all departed with lightened hearts.

Hardly had they done so than telegrams were sent after them forbidding reports of anything they had witnessed, but it was too late to prevent mention in the papers that such a visit had taken place and many tended to give the impression that security concerning actual numbers of bombs destroyed had been breached. In fact nothing of this nature had occurred and the GOC-in-C of Anti-Aircraft Command had specifically told the assembly "The Press are not allowed to publish facts and figures". Even so, the Ministry of Home Security issued a statement on the evening of Wednesday 30 August to the effect that "Detailed information ... is valuable to the enemy and cannot be disclosed to the public at present". This the papers published under such headlines as "Robot toll: No one must tell. Civic chiefs are silenced", but once again the proverbial horse had bolted and some of the visitors had already been approached by reporters. The reactions of the local representatives is interesting, a mayor from south London is alleged to have stated "I had a very interesting and satisfactory demonstration of our defences on Monday, but I do not consider that I have been given authority to divulge figures to anyone" while another is stated to have added "We are not taking any special measures to inform our people". A storm in a tea cup, after nearly five years of war, civic officers, some of whom certainly knew how successful the gunners had been, were far more alert to the dangers of breaking security silence than London gave them credit for!

It goes without saying that the strain on the men and girls too, many of whom were entirely responsible for some of the light guns, was tremendous, and, since Anti-Aircraft Command was already suffering from a series of manpower cuts since the War Office took the view that enemy air activity would in future be minimal, it became necessary to draft in crews from other parts of the country. Perhaps the main contribution to the fatigue which was felt by all, was the lack of sleep which resulted from the necessity to man the guns continually on occasion so that until reinforcements and reliefs could be found, there were times when the actual standard of shooting suffered.

That this state of affairs was quickly altered is shown by figures published a little later which revealed that at the end of the third week of redeployment, the total of flying bombs brought down equalled the 'bag' of the fighters which were themselves hard-pressed, flying a total of twenty thousand interception patrols against the missiles between the opening of the attacks and the first day of September. The peak was achieved during mid-August when no less than fifteen day-fighter and ten night-fighter squadrons were pressed into service against an assault of robots which averaged 102 in a period of twenty-four hours.

Among the unrecorded service men who were under constant stress at this time, must surely be remembered the Duty Reporting Officers in the Command Headquarters Operations Room of the RAF, for the work they had to do was over and above the many responsibilities connected with the invasion of the Continent which was going on at the same time. In order to record and therefore analyse the results of the various aspects of Operation 'Crossbow', Daily Diver Reports were introduced and with this new demand came the formation of a new sub-section of British Intelligence, the Flying Bomb Reporting Section. This, with the introduction by the Nazis of the V-2 rocket, widened its scope to become the Special Intelligence Reporting Section issuing, every twenty-four hours, at 8 a.m. each morning a report for the previous day and night, correct to two hours previously; going as they did to Ministerial and Cabinet level, it was on the information that they supplied that counter-measures were largely based.

The nature of some of the attacks on 'No-ball' targets has already been described in some detail, but the codeword 'Crossbow' covered not only the immediate defence against missiles actually crossing the British coast but also those measures undertaken in the spirit that the finest form of defence is to carry the conflict into the enemy's camp. Therefore it is interesting to note that counter-measures of this type were the subject of the Inter-Departmental Radiolocation (i.e. Radar) Committee meeting as early as March 1944 with a view to looking into the question of day and night attacks against missile targets, not by the conventional methods at that time in use, but with the aid of Oboe and G-H radar systems. The first of these took the form of a ground-controlled blind bombing method, coupled with one for target marking. One of the radar stations would send out a series of signals indicating the track or course to be

121

followed by the bombers while a second would give the time to drop bombs over a target indicator. The G-H system was sometimes referred to as "Oboe in reverse" since it consisted of an airborne transmitter/receiver acting in conjunction with a pair of ground transmitters of the Gee type which were capable of target marking up to a range of about 300 miles, coverage being sufficient for the operation simultaneously of about fifty, specially equipped machines dropping their loads of 500-pound bombs from 10,000 feet or above.

The conclusions of the meeting were that if a mixed force of bombers were despatched, some fitted with Oboe, or dropping-time indicating equipment, the remainder being either individually fitted with G-H gear or led by a machine with this aid on board, a maximum of only 1.5 of the target sites would be seriously damaged in poor weather conditions, even if the force included North American NA-62 Mitchell bombers and the much larger Short Stirling. A rather smaller force, it was calculated, with similar equipment to aid it, could seriously damage a maximum of 5.1 of the targets if there was no increase in known opposition from the target defences and the visibility was good.

7 | Men Again

However ingenious man becomes and no matter how great are his efforts to replace himself by robots, it is one of those strange facets of his mental constitution that sooner or later he returns to the realization that the cheapest guidance system of his weapons, the most readily-available computer, which is also simply maintained and a marvel of miniaturization is his own brain. Thus it was with the flying bomb which, having been designed to meet his dangers for him, man began to use almost as a personal weapon.

At the beginning of July, Southampton had received 20 of a possible 50 missiles launched against her and these were followed by a further bombardment by something under 40 of which a group fell in the region of the aerodrome. Similarly, Gloucester suffered some 20 also, while Manchester received 18, one in the city centre, six nearby and 11 more distantly from a salvo of about 30. Where were they coming from? It was known that other targets than London were envisaged and the salvation of two of these has already been touched upon in another chapter, but it was evident that the later robots were coming from no known launching site and the known range of V-1s were obviously incapable of seeing them across the North Sea.

The answer, it was quickly established, lay in the Nazi's interest in the employment of pick-a-back combinations, several arrangements for which, though probably not intended for the flying bomb, having been noticed recently in reconnaissance photographs.

It seems plain, at this point in time, that the outcome of the Allied Armies' advance into the area where the launching sites were situated was recognized by the Nazis as only a matter of time, so experiments were begun during winter 1943 to investigate the possibilities of air-launching the bombs in an effort to maintain as long as possible Operation *Rumpelkammer*. Although this work, which was carried out at Peenemünde, pre-dated the opening of 'Overlord' it was undertaken in the belief that in the V-1 there still lay a means of ensuring the ports and harbours on the British side of the Channel might be severed from the demands of any invading army which could then be driven out with their supply lines gone, while the bombardment of the towns and cities here would see that the population forced their leaders to sue for peace.

The resultant experiments on the Baltic coast established that the most suitable machine for the work was the well-tried Heinkel He 111H of which the Model 21 was currently being phased, together with the earlier H20 and H16. The method of carrying the bombs was to tuck them under the starboard wing root[1] between the motor and the fuselage in such a way that the port wing of the missile lay behind the undercarriage leg on that side and the rear fuselage and propulsion unit protruded behind the wing of the bomber, to which the sole connection, apart from the twin lugs engaging the lifting lug of the bomb, being an umbilical cord from the jet motor, running to a point under the rearmost of the windows on that side of the bomber.

In order to steady this external load which was slung to the Heinkel's rear spar, a pair of vertical metal struts hung down from the bomber to press on the upper surfaces of the missile's wing some ten centimetres below by means of wooden blocks on the bracing.

In order to release the bomb, the bomb aimer in the parent

---

[1] Reports issued after the interrogation of crews that the missile was carried under the starboard wing are confirmed by photographs, although similar evidence also exists clearly showing a bomb under the port side. To judge from the type of camouflage on the Heinkel, the finish on the missile with its unfaired, external front mounting for the jet motor and above all the fact that the bomber carries a radio call sign and not operational codes, this is a combination used for the early trials of this type of delivery.

machine was seated behind a simple apparatus mounted in a box measuring no more than 20 x 10 centimetres (8 x 4 inches), the crews called it the *Zählwerk*, which had in its centre an illuminated panel presenting a series of six figures in the manner of the mileage recorder in an ordinary car. This panel was duplicated in the observer's position where it lacked the two buttons, one red, one black, and the small lever underneath used to release the missile. The method of doing this took the following form.

At the beginning of the flight, a number, given at briefing, was set on the counter which then automatically ran down to 100 during the journey. With the aircraft at some 1,500 feet (500 metres) the black button, or *Anstellknopf* was pressed to start the motor of the V-1, the *Abstellknopf*, or red stop-button being seldom used. When the counter registered 25, the observer would warn the bomb aimer to stand by and the final release would be made when zero showed on the panel. The crew knew when this had happened by the loss of vibration from the pulse-jet, and the pilot would climb about 300 feet (100 metres) while the bomb would drop for a similar distance before assuming its forward course. Once this was seen to have safely taken place, the bomber would lose height and follow the path of the bomb at some 300 feet, the height at which the outward journey had been made, to confuse any fighters in the vicinity. In the event of an emergency, only the

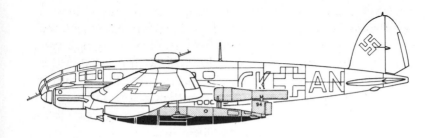

Heinkel 111H-22 with V-1

pilot had means of jettisoning the load, by use of a red lever above his head in the cockpit.

The Heinkel machines used for this work were re-designated He 111H-22s, the conversions being carried out at Oschatz. At the same time, crews were trained in the method of flying with, and releasing the bombs with *Erprobungskommando* Karlshagen at Peenemünde, pilots who had no previous experience with the Heinkel 111 graduating to the Baltic airfield via the transport and communications unit, *Führungsstab der Luftwaffe*. The course at Peenemünde lasted only ten days, the pilots making three flights, each of one hour duration; the first of these being carried out without either crew or missile and were only for final familiarization with the bomber, while the bomb aimers were instructed in the use of the release procedure.

Following this, a second flight was made, this time with a flying bomb underneath, ballasted in lieu of a war-head and with the entire crew on board so that, under the supervision of an instructor, actual experience in releasing the weapon could be gained. The final flight was similar except that no instructor was carried.

Training completed, crews were posted to an operational unit, the sole one at first being a reconstituted III/KG3, the original having been renumbered I/NJG7 the previous March. First operations were flown from Gilze Rijen in Holland, but they were later mounted from Venlo on the Dutch/German border. Here, great secrecy surrounded the operations and the crews were billeted in Grossenkneten village, about five miles distant from the actual flying field at Ahlhorn, which they were not allowed to visit until after dark. All service activities took place away from the field and the office of the *Staffelkapitän* was located near the billets of the crews and even such important training as dinghy drill was carried out dry in the yard of the local inn.

It was not until after dusk had began to fall that they were taken by truck to the airfield where the briefing, consisting of nothing more than the issue of written instructions to the observers and radio operators and a talk on the weather conditions which might be expected, took place. Other members of the crew flew in complete ignorance of these details except for what the observers told them.

When the crews reached the machines, already lined up on the runway, they found that the flying bomb was suspended underneath and hidden by a camouflage net; exactly the same pattern being followed after the return from the sortie when the crews were collected by truck and taken immediately back to the village.

In the late autumn, the early fall of darkness often meant that take-offs began as early as 5 p.m, the aircraft being taxied out at one minute intervals across a fully-lit airfield which had as a guidance beacon a static searchlight at the far edge. Having gained height, the pilot would then set course according to instructions from the observer who directed the flight path along a series of legs close to the Dutch coast, the turning-points being marked by an array of low-powered, visual beacons flashing two-letter Morse combinations that were only switched on for short periods of around ten minutes.

Navigation was entirely by dead reckoning and no aids were available from radio beacons, indeed the radio operators were instructed to use their instruments as little as possible and even the FuGe 101, a radio altimeter was switched on only occasionally to check the readings on the normal, barometric instrument.

For use on this type of operation, the Heinkel bombers had some considerable weight reduction made during modification which was substantially achieved by the removal of the normal bomb racks and the main fuel tank, leaving only the wing tanks wherein was stored sufficient fuel for about five hours.

The elaborate security precautions which demanded that the net hiding the missile remain in place until all the crew was inside the aircraft and therefore unable to see it, was taken to such lengths as deleting the unit's code letters from the side of the fuselage, leaving only the final combination, for example FS, aft of the national marking to distinguish the individual machine and the *Staffel* within the *Gruppe*.

After a while, III/KG3 was redesignated I/KG53 and joined by III/KG53. A temporary pause in the launching programme was brought about between 5 and 15 September when I/KG53 was moved from its Dutch base to Venlo and III/KG53 did not begin operations until the first week of December 1944 and then only by the use of machines hastily withdrawn and modified after service with KG27 the previous September, when the latter unit had been disbanded.

By the time that this type of operation was finally terminated a total of something like 1,200 air-launched flying bombs had been directed at England although the price was high, for the work was not only subject to the normal danger of interception by night fighters but also suffered losses from flying into the sea, brought about by the low altitude at which such flights were made and due to premature explosion of the missiles, in addition to wastage from loss due to engine failure and associated causes.

Naturally attacks of this type and from a new direction had found the East Coast and Midlands without the complex and efficient defences that had been set up in the south, and there was some fear that the attacks, before long, would be extended to the area between Yorkshire and the North Foreland.

As it happened, the Gun Belt was in process of being dismantled at this time due to the manpower cuts introduced in the belief that the enemy had, for a second time, 'shot his bolt', although the Diver Box was to be retained, at least for the moment: some of the Gun Belt weapons even being diverted to reinforce this.

Redeployment was in full swing by the middle of September which was the time of a lull in the air-launched assault while I/KG53 moved, when it became obvious from the suddenly-renewed Heinkel operations that if anything like adequate defence was to be provided, this would have to be taken as far up the east coast as practicable. The decision was therefore taken on 21 September completely to denude the

A Hawker Tempest of 3 Squadron RAF at Newchurch being re-fueled and re-armed. Hawker Tempests brought down a total of 638 V-1s

Early re-deployment deepened the balloon barrage. Here a convoy of these vehicles is seen on the move

A Gloster Meteor 1 of 616 Squadron RAF

Messerschmitt 410s such as this (developed from the earlier Messerschmitt 210) were used to accompany flying bombs on occasion to judge the ranging of the missiles

A typical ROC post. These assisted fighter interception in Operation 'Totter' and supplied operations rooms with the information from which air raid warning officers worked

Although flying bombs were never carried on the back of Heinkel bombers, this 'Brockbank' cartoon reflects the humour of the period

Either STOP the thing or get it UNSTUCK: one or the other—but QUICK !

(*Above*) A flying bomb begins its final dive. (*Below*) A column of smoke marks the explosion in the Drury Lane area

A captured Reichenberg R-IV. The blunt nose is due to the removal of the streamlined cap over the impact fuse

Nordhausen, the *Mittelwerk* in the Hartz Mountains, was captured by the United States Third Armoured Division in April 1945. Found there were many V-1s such as these and also stored V-2s

Reconstruction at the RAE Farnborough
of the first V-2 to fall in Britain

(*Opposite*) A V-2 rocket being prepared
for launching

A civil defence worker poses with a large
section of V-2 rocket

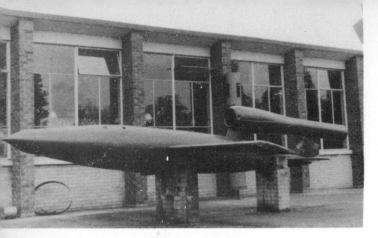

A flying bomb photographed when at the Home Office Training Establishment, Easingwold, now at the Ministry of Technology Establishment at Westcott.

One of the V-1s from the Cosford Aero-Space Museum exhibited by the Hendon RAF Museum at an air display. It has a rather suspect paint finish

A replica flying bomb seen at Old Warden Aerodrome, Bedfordshire, constructed for use in the film *Operation Crossbow*.

south, with the exception of the Diver Box and redeploy all the guns thereby gained up the east coast. Full of confidence, born of the experience gained in the earlier move south, the transfer began the next day. Four days were allowed to complete the operation.

As it turned out, this was to be no repeat of the earlier achievement, for one thing the earlier partial move was incomplete so that guns were scattered in various districts, while for another, transport for the move was fully employed with the changes associated with the Diver Box, while added to this was the time taken to dig up the temporary gun platforms.

The resultant confusion was complete and the gravity of the situation was highlighted on 8 October when General Sir Frederick Pile issued a sharply-worded order pointing out that the aim was to get the guns into action again as quickly as possible, not to waste effort in seeking scapegoats for the chaos, the blame for which must fall on everyone concerned in some measure.

Eighteen days after the scheduled date for conclusion of the move, on 13 October, the change was completed and a Gun Strip, embodying the permanent coastal defences about Yarmouth now ran south to the Diver Box which was not to be changed in shape until February, the following year, the actual new section of the Strip beginning at Southwold.

The form of the Gun Strip was much the same as the old Gun Belt, 5,000 yards wide and extending the same distance out to sea as formerly, but the whole of the resultant gun-defended areas were divided into nine sections covering 1,045 guns of all calibres and searchlight batteries sited at only 3,000 yards spacing in order that they might continuously illuminate V-1s which could appear at as low as 1,000 feet in altitude.

In addition to the anti-aircraft guns, there were, of course, the fighters still, with Mosquitos in prominence since, as has already been stated, the majority of launchings took place after the fall of darkness. In all, about 60 fell to the RAF and

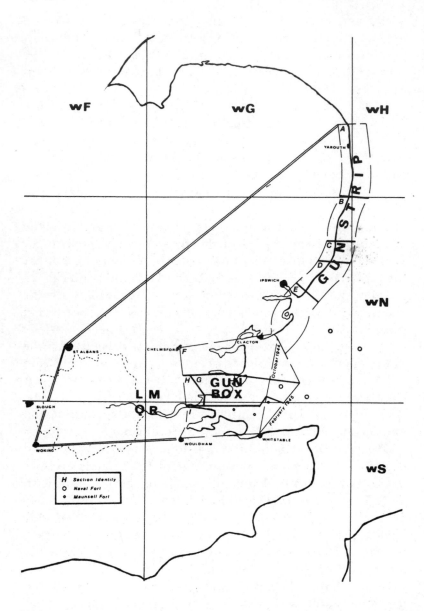

The arrangement of the defences to counter the threat of air-launched flying bombs from the North Sea

roughly half the total of the 638 which actually crossed the coast being brought down by ground fire. From this total, 200 seem to have been directly aimed at London, only 66 getting through.

Although these air-borne launchings finally ceased on 14 January 1945, there were simultaneous attacks by the longer range 'doodle-bugs' already mentioned. These had begun to be sent from Holland on 3 March 1945 and the last one of the 275 sent off did not fall until twenty-five days later at Waltham Cross, together with one companion at Chiselhurst, Kent, but the defences were now so efficient that the anti-aircraft guns only required to be augmented by a single squadron each of Mustang and Tempest fighters.

Meanwhile, the V-1s which were being launched against Antwerp and other parts of the Continent, continued to come, as they had for several months in company with the V-2 rocket. Indeed, during the autumn of 1944, no less than eight anti-aircraft batteries, three of them with mixed crews, had gone from Great Britain to increaes the defences in Belgium just in time, as it turned out for the increased attacks which took place in December coinciding with the Ardennes offensive by the Nazis. These attacks, like their British counterparts also drew to a close in March.

Throughout the V-1 attacks there had been a high level of rivalry among the Nazis, not only between the Army and the Air Force which were responsible for the V-2s and the flying bombs respectively, but also between the services and the SS. The culmination of this took place at the beginning of 1945 when the Nazi Party finally gained control with the entire programme coming under the direction of General Kammler of the SS and the result was cases of V-1s being launched by mixed crews consisting of personnel from the *Luftwaffe* combined with the Waffen SS; Army units alone sending them off, and even cases of launchings for which the SS was responsible but employing *Luftwaffe* crews. Those launched against Continental targets were entirely the responsibility of the Army.

The reintroduction of the human element into the use of flying bombs with security going to such lengths as crews only discovering to what unit they were posted by hearsay, the identity never being written down, was only one aspect of the wide range of uses which the Nazis envisaged for the V-1.

Another was the employment of the new weapon as a piloted bomb. This was no stop-gap introduction brought about by the pressures of the later days of hostilities, but a carefully formulated project which had been occupying the minds of the Nazi leaders since the closing months of 1943. The general idea was that in the, as yet untried missile, lay scope for its development for use against special targets such as heavily-defended military installations on land and warships.

Although this was not a weapon born of desperation, it was the result of the fear of British and American landings being carried out on the Continent of Europe, coupled with a serious depletion of the *Luftwaffe*'s potential.

In order to examine the possibilities more deeply, a special meeting of Deutsche Forschungsinstitut für Segelflug (known as DFS) took place where advice could be taken from various experts. The result of these deliberations was that the most suitable air-frame for attacks by piloted, explosive-carrying aircraft was deemed to be the Messerschmitt 328. This was a low-wing monoplane, originally conceived as a fighter with, on one version an Argus As 109-014 impulse duct, jet motor the power unit of the flying bomb, under each wing. As things turned out the development of this type was not crowned with success and trials with the prototype found the machine subjected to vibration which sadly, caused the death of the test pilot when the air-frame broke up under the stress.

The date was now May 1944 and if the plans were to go ahead as ordered, a new design would have to be found and adapted as quickly as possible. The search for such a type culminated in the selection of the well-tried Focke-Wulf Fw 190 fighter and tests were carried out at the Dedelstorf base of II/KG200's 5th *Staffel*, sometimes known as Kommando

Lange, after its *Staffelkapitän*, Hauptmann Lange, or otherwise the Leonidas *Staffel*. The work took the form of testing the capabilities of the Fw 190 in tremendously steep dives and manoeuvres which subjected the type to maximum 'g', all with a large bomb, impact fused, underneath. Although these tests were not unproductive there was reckoned to be little hope of such machines piercing the defences with the weight penalty of the explosive, although another model was developed for the carriage of a 940 kilogramme (2,090 pounds) torpedo. Added to this was the fact that, with the set-back to the Messerschmitt design there seemed little hope of it being of use, so that the DFS was faced with a serious dilemma.

Credit for the solution must go to SS-Hauptsturmführer Otto Skorzeny who came up with the idea of a modified form of the V-1 missile and work was begun immediately. In the remarkably short time of only fourteen days, the DFS produced no less than four models all based on the original robot, which were later to be identified by the designations R-I; RII; R-III and R-IV after the adoption of the codename 'Reichenberg'.

Trials began in September at Lärz and immediately ran into difficulties. The converted air-frames were carried aloft by a Heinkel He III, fitted with a rack underneath, and the first met with disaster when a crash was brought about by the premature loss of the canopy from the missile, while the second attempt fared no better. Thereafter development flying was entrusted to a pair of pilots from Rechlin, Flugkapitän Hanna Reitsch, chosen for her petite stature which would fit comfortably into the cramped cockpit, and Heinz Kensch, together with Otto Skorzeny. Even so, the work was not without its hazards and a case occurred where a tailplane was damaged against the fuselage of the Heinkel parent-machine and another when a missile become almost uncontrollable when the ballast broke loose. The most serious accident took place at a slightly later date when Hanna Reitsch was seriously injured during trials from a dolly. This mobile holding-crutch had been taken from a Messerschmitt Me 163B and on take-off it refused to part company from the bomb, but although by and large these weapons handled satisfactorily enough in the air, the high speeds made landing dangerous.

The first three variants of the basic design were all intended as trainers, the R-I was a single-seat model with no motor but a landing skid and flaps were fitted. Very similar was the R-II which, in the forward compartment occupied by ballast in the earlier version was a second cockpit, glazed, like the standard one aft, with a single-piece hood. The fin and rudder areas were also enlarged and, once again, no propulsion unit of any form was fitted. The R-III resembled in all but detail the operational model and was powered by the same type of motor as that fitted to the original robot design: like the others it was a trainer, but of an advanced sort with a landing skid, flaps and ballast in lieu of the war-head. Like all 'Reichenberg' variants, it was fitted with ailerons, unlike the unmanned original. These were fitted aft of the trailing edge of the standard wing. The operational type was almost exactly similar except that a war-head was fitted and on some, a simple form of foresight was found, evidently intended to assist in aiming towards the target. Many photographs show this type with what appears to be a flattened extremity to the nose, but in fact it is the final streamlined dome which is missing and acted as a cap to the impact fuse.

Inside, the cockpit was sparsely fitted, the seat consisting of no more than a ply bucket with a small, padded head-rest. Rudimentary too, was the instrumentation, consisting of, from left to right, only an arming switch for rendering the war-head 'live', a clock, airspeed indicator, altimeter and turn and bank indicator; while below, on the floor was a compass and 24 volt wet battery to the right and a hood jettison lever on the pilot's left. Telephone communication was possible between the pilot of the bomb and that of the carrier until the moment of release, but there was no radio.

Internal modifications consisted of the removal of those components rendered redundant by a human guidance system, including the retention of only one of the two spherical compress air bottles formerly carried, this for the pressurization of the fuel tank. Modifications of the standard robot were undertaken at a special plant hidden in the woods of Dannenberg, although there was another at Pulverhof. Here, apart from the changes already listed, the war-heads for operational models, about 175 being produced, were of a slightly changed form, consisting of a long truncated cone covered by a wooden fairing after the manner of those of the longer-range robot bombs.

Much has been written about the likelihood of the pilot surviving a sortie of this kind, the idea being stated that he was expected to aim the bomb for the final part of its journey, jettison the hood, and then bale out using his back-parachute. In order to examine fully, this question, it is first necessary to look at the altitude of the Karlshagen Establishment, the research station at Peenemünde. This refused to have anything to do with the idea and it was not until it became the responsibility of the Ainring-based DFS that any progress was made. The initial work was carried out fairly openly under the guise of preparing a machine from which aerodynamic observations could be made, the results being later applied to improved versions of the V-1 robot.

When it became obvious that the work was nothing of the sort, there was ample evidence of the provision for the pilot to escape but there remains the problem of whether this was a practical possibility since, as far as is known, no trials were conducted into this aspect of the work, so that it becomes necessary to look into the procedure involved to find an answer. The canopies of operational 'Reichenberg' bombs were designed to slide forward to permit the pilot to climb in, but to jettison, they were flung open to starboard and it was not until an angle of forty-five degrees had been reached that they could fall away and it seems more than likely that this would not have taken place cleanly due to the air pressure occasioned by the speed of the dive towards the target, which might have been in excess of 400 m.p.h. since the design fault in the original, robot flying bomb had now been corrected and the missile no longer lost impulsion when the motor stopped and was driven at, rather than falling on the target, an improvement also incorporated in the basic form of bomb by this time. Additionally, even if the hood did fall away as planned, the pilot would have had to compete with this same blast of air tending to prevent his escape across the height of the jet unit immediately aft of his position, risking injury from the tailplane in doing so for it must be remembered that as early as the Battle of Britain, four years previously, pilots were finding it necessary to anticipate the ejector seat by, in some cases, turning their fighters over in order to ensure that they were flung out by gravitational pull when escaping by parachute.

One is left with the question of whether the volunteer pilots were aware of these debatable points, that they were is amply demonstrated by the applied title of *Selbstopfermänner* or suicide men. This makes nonsense of the cover story that the machines were being prepared for no more than trial work, which, in itself could be construed as an admission that something distasteful to the European mind was envisaged, although the provision of the parachute gave to all concerned a mental provision that the odds in favour of survival were something of a higher order than the facts indicated. A terrible reflection on the ultimate effect of politics when their insidious poison erodes the civilizing effect of hundreds of years until they breed blind, cold-blooded fanaticism.

This having been said, there were, nevertheless, great attractions in the weapon for the minds of many members of the Nazi Party who still hoped to snatch victory out of defeat and use the 'R-weapons' against troop concentrations at the various bridgeheads, and to this end some thirty members of the SS, all picked for their depth of indoctrination, were trained as pilots. A companion programme was begun for the crews of conventional machines within KG200, which would act as parent aircraft for delivery.

Against all this it must be stated in fairness that a strong element in German government and military circles refused to take the scheme seriously. It had never been a particularly large project and even in its earliest days when enthusiasm was at its height, the team which had produced three modified bombs from original 'doodle-bugs' in the actual working time of only three days, had consisted of only eighteen men, fifteen technicians and three engineers.

The real end to the whole bizarre scheme began gradually in October 1944 when a new Geschwader Kommodore was appointed to KG200 in the form of Werner Baumbach who favoured the several alternative schemes involving expendable explosive-carrying machines without crews and the whole idea rapidly faded away. Over two decades later, however, there were tales in circulation, and it is doubtful if they were ever anything more than that, of the thirty *Selbstopfermänner*, frustrated by the non-availability of converted missiles in time to attack Allied troopships used in connection with Operation 'Overlord', refusing alternative targets as unworthy of the demands entailed; while history remembers Otto Skorzeny more for his choice by Hitler to plan the attempted snatch of the Italian dictator, Benito Mussolini from imprisonment in an hotel, 6,500 feet up the Gran Sasso mountain range in central Italy in the previous September than for anything else.

When the Allied Armies finally penetrated into Nazi-held Europe, many examples of the 'R-weapons' were found almost intact, including the greater part of the stock of Reichenberg IVs, said to number under 200, which British Intelligence was quick to dub V-4, knowing, as it did, about the existence of the sinister V-3 which is described in a later chapter. Discovered also, were several complete R-II, twin-seat trainers with only minor damage inflicted to the plastic canopies by the retreating Nazis when they abandoned the assembly plant at Pulverhof to advancing American troops. The existence of these, coupled with the number of operational weapons found, was taken to indicate that, until the programme was allowed to lapse, a continuous training scheme was planned as, indeed, would be called for when it is realized that the first batch of pilots were the successful ones from an intake of seventy volunteers, indicating a high rejection rate for a variety of reasons.

As we have seen, the two attempts to introduce a human element into the operation of what was originally seen as an entirely automatic form of warfare met with only limited success but the third field of experiment was based on firmer ground, namely the possibility of using towed flying bombs.

The idea of a load-carrying trailer for aircraft was by no means new and trials had been carried out in Germany as early as five years previously. The advantage of such a system was that the load of a machine could be increased without making undue demands on the lift and as applied to the military field it could well be the answer to the delivery of bombs to a distant target without endangering the crew and the expensive equipment represented by the parent tug machine.

The initial suggestion for such a field of research came from the Arado company of Brandenburg, so it is hardly surprising that the tug should be one of their own products, namely the Arado Ar 234B, a twin-jet reconnaissance-bomber, fitted with Junkers Jumo 004 gas turbines, which had only gone into production in June 1944 and thus became the third type of Nazi jet-propelled aircraft to see operational service, albeit in small numbers, on the Western Front.

For the tests, which were conducted at Rechlin, specially modified flying bombs were used consisting of the basic model with the impulse-duct motor unit removed and replaced by a streamlined fairing for the anti-spin parachute above the fin and rudder. The tailplane too, was removed. Other modifications consisted of fitting a large, spatted undercarriage braced by means of struts to the fuselage sides below the wing: these wheels were automatically jettisoned soon after take-off. Between these fairings was a very large ventral bulge from the front of which protruded the towing bar.

Had the experiments been concluded, and it was only the end of the war which prevented the operational use of the weapon, the fairing for the parachute, which was only intended to reduce the landing speed of the test-vehicle, would have been dispensed with and a motor fitted so that to all intents the trailer would have been a conventional V-1 with a disposable undercarriage, although it seems probable that a dolly might have been used on one form or another, while the tow bar would have been shed once the weapon had been taken to within range of its target, pointed onto the requisite course and cast off.

So far, we have seen that the Nazis regarded the flying bomb as capable of a considerable amount of development which would probably have been pursued into other channels had its comparatively late introduction not prevented this due to the end of hostilities. It is of considerable interest that this attitude was shared by the Allies as well, the first of whom, the United States, was quick to look into the possibilities.

The first announcement of this took place during October 1944 and the British public learned of it via their newspapers at the beginning of the following month. "A number of factories," ran one report, "including aircraft factories, in the USA have been turned over to the production of reaction-propelled flying bombs. These missiles are similar to their German counterparts, but incorporate several modifications. At least two thousand are being built." Reaction was as sharp as it was immediate: some optimists mentally rejected the idea, saying that it was no more than a propaganda exercise designed to alarm the Nazis, others took the line that frightful weapons of this type had no place in the armoury of the Allies and that in any hands the use of these bombs was "stupid, wasteful and pointless" as there was no shortage of bomber pilots who could select military targets. Others pointed out that the whole effort was a waste as the bombs would never be used up before final victory was achieved, although these people took no account of the fact that some reports stated that the missiles were for use against Japan where victory in the immediate future seemed less certain. There were other reactions also, never expressed in print or on the radio but expressed in private; perhaps the Americans were not the demi-gods which the Allied propaganda presented them as being, perhaps they were no better than the Nazis, while wiser counsels suggested that men were just human beings and much the same all the world over.

Assuming that the new flying bombs were to be directed at Japan, "to keep the number of prisoners as low as possible" as one correspondent put it, there was bewilderment in public circles as to how they were to be delivered, since at this time the average person was still vague about the problems associated with air launching, although they would have been relieved to know that the Nazi attempts to do this, now becoming increasingly sporadic, were suffering from fuel shortages which would increase until it strangled the programme.

On the other side of the Atlantic, reaction was naturally different among a people who had never been on the receiving end of this or any other type of attack and news-reels were shown at cinemas of the test programme, while specimens were exhibited to representatives of the Press. The general appearance of the bombs thus seen, differed but little from their Nazi counterparts although there were some external modifications which included a different pattern of forward mounting of the jet-motor, and reporters were told that the type was being mass-produced by the Ford Motor Company's factories with the Detroit plant concentrating on propulsion units, facts which gave the first clue to their design source as, up to this period, they had been referred to only as 'Americanised V-1s' until the correct designation of Ford JB-2 was released.

It so happened that at the same moment in time as the Nazi weapon was to appear in operational service, American military thinking was following exactly the same lines and for some time before the first use of V-1s, the possibilities of using redundant B-17 and B-24 bombers, packed with high explosive and radio controlled, had been examined in the United States. Then came the Nazi weapon and having begun to consider copying it as early as June 1944, the final decision was taken at the beginning of the following month and the War Department authorized ninety million dollars for the work, known as Project MX-544.

In the event, there was a school of thought which believed that an entirely new concept would give better results and the Northrop Aircraft organization looked into the possibilities of a twin-engined flying bomb, powered with a pair of pulse-jet units based by Fords on the Argus motor.

The resultant air-frame was of the flying wing pattern, constructed from magnesium and aluminium and with a wing span of 30 feet (9 metres) making it capable of delivering a load of explosive in the region of 3,700 pounds (1,678 kilogrammes) despite the later decision to power it with only a single motor.

Designated the JB-1A, flight trials discovered serious control problems while a parallel project resulting in the JB-10 met with no greater success since it proved too complex and consequently expensive for an expendable weapon.

Simultaneous with this work, the Republic Aircraft Corporation was content to be less ambitious and was simply constructing a copy of the V-1, based on examination of several wrecked specimens which were specially flown from Great Britain in United States transport aircraft; the first arriving as early as 9 July at Wright Field where a team was waiting to examine the parts and to re-create the FZG 76. So well did they do their work that only seventeen days later saw the emergence of a complete American copy of the Argus pulse jet incorporating original German and copied parts, the work of the Ford Motor Company. This, united with the Republic produced air-frame was subjected to wind tunnel tests at the same Air Force base, work which carried on throughout October and into the first days of November, in fact during the period when the existence of these copy missiles was being announced as an accomplished fact by the news media.

At the same time as the test programme was in full swing, a second line of development was tackling the question of launching. At that period very few details were available on how this was done to the prototypes in France, beyond the fact that some form of ramp was employed to launch the missiles at an angle in the region of five degrees. After consultations with the Monsanto Chemical Company, which was capable of supplying solid fuel booster rockets able to move a form of sledge with a combined static thrust of 4,000 pounds (1,814 kilogrammes) with the JB-2 flying bomb mounted above, experimental firings along a three-rail track inclined at six degrees to the horizontal were carried out at what was then known as Muroc Dry Lake in the Californian Mojave Desert, (later, Edward's Air Force Base). These proved entirely successful and it was 12 October when, by dint of day and night work there, coupled with round-the-clock activity at Florida's Eglin Field where mock-up 'No-ball' sites had been constructed for further study in the 'Crossbow' field, that the first American 'doodle bug' was sent aloft. Its behaviour was strangely familiar to that of the Nazi original when first test fired, for although the missile certainly left the rails and dropped its sledge, a considerably larger and clumsier item than the steam-driven piston on the Walter ramp, it crashed only a short distance away before the reason for the mishap could be determined. Indeed, despite the meticulous copy which the American design was, even down to dimensional similarity to within a few inches and a near-exact employment of the wing aerofoil with the adoption of NACA 0015 section, it required something in the region of fifty test launches before the programme gave any hope of success. Even so, the pressures of war had meant that production models had gone ahead at Republic's assembly plant and a large stock of JB-2s was available, all fitted with the Ford IJ-15-1 motor, but it was not until the New Year of 1945 that the first operational versions began to be delivered.

Although considerable ingenuity had gone into the production of a means of launching the missiles from a fixed site, it was obvious that their range precluded anything of this sort being employed for sending the flying bombs to a target as far distant as the Japanese islands. So the Nazi weapon was once again taken as prototype and trials conducted on the lines of the Heinkel-borne launchings but with a pair of bombs suspended under each wing of a B-17 which released them towards the target at 5,000 feet (1,524 metres), about three times that at which the V-1s were sent off. Air launches from B-29s and from a dorsal crutch on B-24s were dropped, but experiments continued from the 'Flying Fortress' and of the ten dropped in the spring of 1945 from machines operating out of Wendover, Utah, four were successful, and at a later date the B-29 trials were revived.

With the sudden termination of the war, the United States, found herself in possession of 1,200 Ford JB-2s for which she had no use and no operational experience. Although the project was not immediately stopped against the possibility of the data being applicable to the use of unmanned atomic missiles which was then being examined, as events turned out it was the United States Navy and not the Army, who had done the lion's share of the work, which made use of the Ford flying bomb.

The decision to continue the programme was announced on 12 March 1946, authorization to convert two Gato-class submarines, the S.S.337, *Carbenero* and S.S.348, *Cusk* to carry flying bombs having been given one week earlier, while AVM-1 *Norton Sound* was pressed into service as a guided weapon vessel soon after. Eleven months later, 12 February 1947 saw the first actual firing take place from a submarine when *Cusk* sent off a Naval Ford JB-2, now designated a LTV-N-2 'Loon' and a KUW-1 a little earlier, while cruising on the surface off Point Mugu. By the time the exercises off the same point were carried out in May, three years later, all three vessels had fired several such missiles which now had the refinement that it was possible to control them towards their target in flight. The process of launching and subsequent guidance took the form of the submarine first surfacing and the crew opening the small watertight hangar where the 'Loon' was stored. It was then assembled and the whole vessel aligned towards the target, the bomb was sent off on its journey. At first, flight control was undertaken by a ground station if the target was more than about 50 miles (80 kilometres) distant, but the day arrived when the submarine could launch a 'Loon', submerge again and guide its spawn for the entire journey up to a maximum distance of something like twice the first figure, thus ushering in the Vought Regulus and Martin Matador missiles by sea and on land, of the 1950s.

This was the high-water mark of the career of the 'American buzz bomb' and makes the original reaction something of a storm in a teacup for the rumours that they were being issued in massive numbers to the United States Navy proved without foundation and the type was never used in anger by them or the Army. But there was one side-effect to all this; hundreds of millions of dollars were wasted at a slightly later date in an abortive attempt, known as Project Navaho, to perfect a flying bomb fitted with a nuclear warhead from the basis of the Nazi design.

As with all things new, other countries than the United States were anxious to exploit the basic idea of a robot missile for their own use, and twelve years later one could still see over the firing ranges of France, what were, quite obviously 'doodle bugs' complete even to the pulse unit set high on the rear fuselage. The name of the motor had changed, it was now termed a ramjet, but the only difference in external appearance of the little aircraft was the provision of outrigged, twin fins and rudders. There was one important difference, however. The Arsenal 5.501 as it was called, was under remote control from the ground by means of radio as befitted an aerial target. Remembering the cover-name adopted for the British experiments in the field of flying bombs during the first European conflict, as detailed in Chapter One of this book, it might almost be said that the wheel had come full circle!

8 | Death from the Stratosphere

The wet and miserable summer of 1944 was drawing towards its close when a hopeful headline appeared in the newspapers, "The end of V-1" it announced and added "while V-2 may never start". But Mr Duncan Sandys struck a more cautious note at a Press conference where the first question was on the subject of V-2, "I am a little chary of talking about V-2", he replied, adding, "we do know quite a lot about it." Speaking at Birmingham on 10 September, Lord Dudley had reason to warn his audience of grimmer things to come when he remarked, "It is possible, even probable, that the enemy will be able to launch something else at a longer range and a different type from V-1. Therefore, it is necessary for us to be on our guard."

In fact the first of the new weapons had already fallen on London on 7 September, three days previously, but there followed an unbidden conspiracy of silence among the population who began, under this new threat, to look back almost with nostalgia to the days of the flying bomb as they had done at the beginning of their use to the onslaught by conventional bombers four summers before. At their back doors, all attention after the peculiar double bang which marked the fall of another rocket in the area, suburban housewives would ask each other, "I wonder what that was?" and receive the reply, "Oh! it's *one of those*." In other districts, different euphemisms and reference would be made to "Another gasworks blown up".

The exact form of 'Retaliation Weapon Number 2' was in some doubt in the mind of the public at large and also in that of the Press which guided it. There were references to flying bombs of greatly increased range which could be launched from inside Germany, to a super-long-range gun and, nearer the truth, to a rocket shell. This is how it was described in reports reaching this country from Berne which based their information on propaganda leaflets dropped on Nazi-held Milan informing the population that V-2 was about to be put into action. Neutral Stockholm too provided an outlet for the flood of warnings which heralded the rocket as they had V-1.

The first districts to feel the teeth of this new form of bombardment were in the Epping Forest area and it was reported as the arrival of flying bombs, a deception which fooled few who had ever heard the roar of a heavy shell exploding but was accepted by people who realized the importance of failing to confirm the arrival of the V-2. So the 'flying gasometer' it became despite the obvious conclusions to be drawn from the visit to the 'incident' by the Minister of Home Security, Mr Herbert Morrison in company with Admiral Sir Edward Evans, later Lord Mountevans and popularly known as 'Evans of the Broke' in his capacity of Regional Commissioner for Civil Defence.

"Blimey, look out mate!" cried a workman from a hole in the road to a passer-by who, instantly but too late spun round as a double report rent the air and the pavement shook under his feet. Then, just as suddenly there was nothing to see except a white vapour trail hanging vertically in the air, already being blown into a blurred shape by the wind at altitude while to meet it climbed a billowing cloud of black-brown smoke from the devastation a few miles away. That is how the rocket struck, without warning and from the peak of its trajectory some fifty miles up. Its outpaced sound so marked its arrival by a double boom, the first, a sonic one, the other the explosion of the one-ton war-head.

To discover the genesis of *Vergeltung 2* it is necessary that a search be made as far back as 1933, the year of Hitler's rise to power. Before this there had existed in Germany a research organization, the Raketenflugplatz or VfR dedicated to the study of rockets, not so much for their military potential but in the interests of pure science although the interplanetary possibilities were realized even at that time. However, the international connections of the VfR were frowned on by the Gestapo and the body was closed down and its use of the former Army ammunition depot suspended.

The driving force behind this society, the twenty-year-old Wernher von Braun, was thus faced in 1943 with a sudden cessation of the funds which had been flowing in and so, in order to complete experimental work on the thesis which could gain him a doctorship, the young man found himself working on rockets for the Army.

The first of these was termed the Aggregate 1 which explains the terminology of later rockets and the familiar designation of A-4 to the 1944 weapon, but the pioneer experiments proved a failure since the missile, powered by the explosive mixture of oxygen in liquid form and alcohol, which a humorous writer was later to describe as a "wicked waste", exploded on ignition.

Two fresh attempts were made that year from the launching ramp on the island of Borkum, over the North Sea and both were sufficiently successful in reaching some two miles altitude that the Army immediately made grants to enable further work to go ahead on a new form of very much larger rocket. Mindful of the trouble which had destroyed the A-1, new fuel flow valves had been introduced and such innovations as launching without a ramp, the missile being supported on its fins alone at ignition, as was the wartime weapon, and the addition of a green dye to stain the sea of the target area and thus assist recovery marked a much more sophisticated design. Indeed it was just this degree of advancement that was to be the undoing of the A-3 because the parachute, intended to let the rocket down without damage, suddenly slipped after launching and was instantly burnt up by the efflux. The progress of the missile immediately became erratic, it began to spin and fell into the ocean. No greater success attended subsequent launchings despite the elimination of the parachute and it became obvious that the whole design would have to be rethought.

Strangely, the modified design was termed the A-5 and turned out to be smaller than its predecessor from which it inherited an important feature in that the combustion chamber was contained wholly inside the rear fuel tank. Its general appearance resembled a miniature V-2 mainly in that the fins protruded considerably to each side of the body whereas those of the A-3 had only slightly broken the vertical contour.

Also introduced at this time were steerable vanes of carbon set in the exhaust blast. These consisted of plates of surprisingly small area, fireproof to withstand a temperature of only a little under 3,000°C from the exhaust gases. On the wartime A-4 these were augmented by small aerodynamic-section rudders.

With the Nazi regime now firmly established in Germany and the military potential realized by the Army authorities, in addition to the prestige value for the Party, finance became easier and this speeded up the experimental work which was still being pursued by Dr von Braun in the belief that he was expanding the boundaries of man's knowledge by giving him access to the solar system rather than perfecting a weapon of war, so that it was in a sense of welcoming in the Space Age that the launchings, again over the Baltic from the small island of Griefswalder Oie, of the A-5 rocket took place in the summer of 1938 while the Czechoslovakian crisis was yet gathering speed in Europe. These launchings were completely successful from the first and took the form of firing the new missiles without any guidance system fitted, up to an altitude of about eight miles before a parachute was ejected to bring the rocket back to earth once more a few hundred yards off shore. Thus it was that the same A-5s were used several times over, some being fired from platforms which tilted them to extend the trajectory.

By the time that the Nazi *Luftwaffe* was fighting the Battle of Britain in the summer skies of 1940 two important steps had taken place in the progress of the von Braun rocket programme. The first was that a new site had been selected for further experiments. Once more on the Baltic coast this was situated near to the village of Peenemünde between Stettin and Bergen to its north. Here it was possible to set up a series of launching pads, engineering workshops, staff and army barracks and test stands all with the services of a dock and railway; later on this was augmented by a Russian P.O.W. camp to provide labour for road and other constructional work. The other important change was that with the setting up of a wind tunnel at the new centre about eighteen months before the outbreak of hostilities it became possible to examine the likelihood of designing the rocket with a view to its employment as a type of heavy artillery, and consequently work was begun on an enlarged version of the A-5 to be termed the A-4, measuring forty-two feet in length. In this the provision of a combustion chamber separate from the rearmost fuel tank had been reverted to, despite the restriction which movement by road and the necessity of negotiating bridges and overhead obstructions placed on the size of the weapon. In consequence it was possible to provide a war-head containing only a ton of explosive and representing about one seventh of the total length. Even so with the combined force of being driven into its target by the rocket motor and the acceleration of a drop of several miles to combine in an approach speed of 3,500 miles per hour, or about seven times the speed of sound, the limited explosive force was capable of blasting a crater of impressive dimensions with extensive, if local devastation at its maximum range of some 170 miles so that Greater London easily came within its operating radius, a fact which impressed Hitler. Indeed it may have been an early realization of the hostile capabilities of the rocket experiments that prompted him to boast in a speech calling on Great Britain to make peace, made only a fortnight after the outbreak of war "We have a weapon which is not yet known and with which we ourselves cannot be attacked," and Dr R.V. Jones in his report on the possible types of weapon in the

Nazi armoury had specifically mentioned long range guns and rockets.

But the operational employment of this type of thing was still in the future when the first A-4 lifted off. It was 1942 and the resultant projectile represented a combined result from aerodynamicists, rocket engineers and combustion experts who had developed the propulsion motor separately. Hopes were high among the watchers as the great cylinder slowly lifted off; only to be dashed as the fins took the weight again as it settled back onto them and, with their collapse, fell over on to its side and destroyed itself in an explosion followed by a sheet of flame. No greater success attended the attempt four weeks later when there was speculation as to the behaviour of the rocket once it reached the speed of sound but it achieved nothing approaching this velocity since it became unstable shortly after launching and broke up above the firing pad.

The incorporation of the modifications dictated by these mishaps delayed further tests until the beginning of October when the missile behaved exactly as planned.

It would have been strange if the resultant activity at Peenemünde had gone unnoticed by British Intelligence since the Ministry of Armaments and War Production had immediately put in hand with the von Braun team plans both for the further development of launching and guidance as well as production on a large scale at a nearby site. Elsewhere assembly was undertaken at the old Zeppelin airship hangars, useful due to their size, at Friedrichshafen and at a new factory on the outskirts of Vienna: so that it was possible only nine months later for accurate maps to be drawn in this country of the whole of the Peenemünde complex based on the large number of reconnaissance photographs which the RAF had built up from the sorties of single, unarmed machines often polished for greater speed and taking great risks in the task.

The site was consequently singled out for the attentions of Bomber Command the crews of which, at the briefing had the various buildings and quarters identified but were not informed of the nature of the target, it being implied that experimental radar work was being carried out there. They were, however, left in no doubt as to the importance of destroying the installation since a special message was read out from the A.O.C.-in-C. of Bomber Command, (then) Air Marshal Arthur Harris which contained the warning "The extreme importance of this target and the necessity of achieving its destruction with one attack is to be impressed on all crews".

On the night of 17 August 1943, five hundred and ninety heavy bombers with Pathfinders took off to launch Operation 'Hydra'. This was the first occasion when the master bomber technique had been used on a large scale and also the first use of the 'red fire spot' marker bomb operationally. This was an interesting device consisting of a 250-pound bomb case into which was packed cotton wool impregnated to burn for some ten minutes; set to burst at 3,000 feet it bathed the target area in a great red light for the bomb aimers to work by.

The plan was to deceive the defences over the target area by following a route which might have indicated that the goal be either Stettin or Berlin and before it became obvious that it was neither the fire glow was swamping the experimental station in its light. So successful was the deception that night fighters were standing by to repulse an attack on the Berlin district so that anti-aircraft guns alone had to deal with the raiders over Peenemünde: but in the forty minutes which followed when incendiaries and high explosive cascaded down by the light of an almost full moon, the guns did their work only too well, backed up by the night fighters which were finally diverted when the real intention of the attack became obvious, they accounted with the guns for forty of the British bombers. Even so successive waves of attackers poured their loads onto the target with special attention to the barracks which were supposed to house the technicians so that a communiqué issued the following morning could claim seeming success when "Last night a strong force of our bombers attacked Peenemünde".

The final wave of bombers left the target three hours after the sirens had first sounded and left behind them a scene of destruction which only became wholly evident when a cold, grey dawn climbed out of the Baltic to herald 18 August; all around was a scene of chaos which stank with the smell of the fine dry dust from the ruined buildings and the task began of creating some order out of the ruin.

One of the first things which became evident was that the death toll was nothing even approaching the five thousand believed by the Allies, which would have represented some seventy per cent of the total work force; instead the casualties were nearer eight hundred, about half of which were among the construction gangs formed from prisoners of war. The Nazi dead were said to include General Jeschonnek and General von Chamier-Glisezenski but in fact the only key scientific man lost was the propulsion expert Dr Walter Thiel.

The material damage too, was far greater to the domestic quarters and the workshops where wind-tunnel models were prepared than to the aerodynamic section and the buildings housing the guidance system manufacture, so that much of the important work could go ahead again in a few days time with very little interruption.

But although the rocket was an untried form of warfare the raid had taught a lesson to Hitler who immediately ordered the excavation of underground assembly shops at Nordhausen south of the Harz Mountains, providing just what was lacking at the Baltic base and which might have easily meant the total destruction of several years work, an indestructible factory safe from air attack; this was the *Mittelwerk*, in a series of forty-nine tunnels cut in the soft rock.

Considerable thought was then given to the problem of launching the new missiles in an offensive role which would, in turn, affect the training schemes to which the first production missiles now coming off the assembly line at a rate of about eighty per week were being directed. The immediate reaction was to set up enormous launching platforms protected by huge thicknesses of concrete, but finally more advanced tactical thinking prevailed and the firing batteries took the form of highly mobile units which could make maximum use of natural cover such as could be found in the thickly wooded areas of the Continent. Although this was all very well in theory it meant that no fixed equipment could be installed by which to raise the A-4, which had to travel in a horizontal position, into the upright, weighing, as it did, over twelve tons, fuelled and ready for firing. After much deliberation it was decided that the answer lay in the provision of a transporter which, by means of a lifting arm could raise the rocket up leaving only the necessity to charge the tanks from mobile tankers, place in position a protective cone between the fins to prevent the exhaust flames from being deflected and damaging the rear of the missile, and align the V-2 with the target.

With these problems solved an intensive programme of operational training began during the summer of 1944 while the flying-bomb attacks were still getting into their stride over southern England. From these it quickly became evident that even now, all was not well with the design since over half of those launched were breaking up in the air from the stresses of flutter which began at an altitude of about two miles and there was some delay while the body design was strengthened.

While all this was going on, launching areas were being prepared in northern France; this work began somewhat late since orders had already been given to begin building massive concrete emplacements such as were originally thought to be called for. It was these which excited the interest of many Press representatives who examined them immediately after the areas were taken by Allied troops following the invasion of Europe. They took the form of gigantic bunkers sited as far as possible to make maximum use of the natural camouflage from which the rockets would have been rolled ready for firing, up a ramp protected by curving walls of green concrete, ten feet thick and covered at the lower level by a canopy of concrete and steel, sixteen feet thick. Frequently these bunkers were set into hill sides to make detection increasingly difficult, while within, a series of tunnels made a labyrinth of workshops where the missiles could be prepared almost immune from attack. Once this was done the final stage of the V-2's journey was via a mammoth 'waiting room' at the foot of the ramp: this measured something like ten yards square with walls three feet thick and closed by steel doors two feet in thickness. Into this chamber the commander could look at the final preparations through a slit in comparative comfort very different from the cramped accommodation of an armoured car where the commander of a mobile unit found himself. Transportation up the ramp was by railway with the missiles supported by means of their fins on a series of trucks and it was these rails which gave the impression to visiting journalists that the complex was designed to serve some sort of super flying bomb.

One of these bunkers is on record as having been concealed beneath the fortifications of a site dating from the time of Louis XIV near Cherbourg and the work of his military engineer Vauban. It had been strengthened by Napoleon and then prepared for twentieth-century warfare by Hitler's slave labour but was abandoned, unfinished when the vulnerability of such an installation system became evident. A fate which also met an alternative design which demanded that the rockets be taken to the roof of the preparation bunker on a type of lift and aligned and fired from there.

By the end of August 1944 the major problems associated with the A-4 had all been solved and fresh plans were going ahead to perfect a development of the A-2 fitted with wings giving it the appearance of having been sired by a V-1. Due to the speed involved these were swept back and a set of steerable rudders fitted to augment the carbon vanes. In theory these should have achieved an altitude of something like seventy miles at the zenith of their trajectory before descending to some thirty-seven miles and flying on a dropping course to the target. Indeed, a pair of these A-4b rockets had been constructed and test-fired but only one had shown any signs of success and in any case it was obvious that the development programme would be too lengthy for consideration under the worsening situation into which Nazi Germany now found herself plunged.

After all the years of experiment and work the first V-2 was launched against London on 7 September 1944, the date is not without its irony since on the previous day, the Home Secretary who was also Minister of Home Security, Mr Herbert Morrison had thought it proper to announce that "The Battle of London is won", certainly the lash had been taken out of the V-1 attacks by this time and the newspapers were making much of the fact that it was eighty-two hours since the last flying bomb, but one reporter introduced a sober note when he added "As a precaution the Civil Defence service, the Home Guard and fire guards will continue to be on the alert for a time".

The first of the rockets fell at Chiswick and the other fired that day caused devastation at Epping. This was a long way from the fifteen per day which Hitler had been informed *each battery* could fire, but they were the heralds not only of four thousand launched at Antwerp as well as London but also ushered in the missile age.

As has been foreshadowed, quite a quantity of information was now to hand about the second 'Retaliation Weapon'. As in the case of the flying bomb much of this had been carefully assembled by Dr R.V. Jones who with great patience had applied his scientific mind to the questions of military intelligence to such a degree that he was able to estimate from the fragments pieced into the mosaic not only the range and destructive power of the missile but with uncanny accuracy guess at the possible production total which a few days before the first attack stood at 1,800, ready for firing by Lehr und Versuchs Artillerie Batterie Nr 444 and Nr 485 in the Friesland district, although they were later moved back, the latter to Munster.

First-hand familiarity now proved it a very inaccurate weapon its main characteristic being that it arrived without warning at a speed greater than that of sound so that no form of defence was thought possible and therefore lives were needlessly lost by civilians who had been unable to seek shelter.

Typical of the sort of tragedy which had to be endured was that wrought ten days after the opening of the attack on the London area; it was a Sunday morning and lunch was being prepared in the many suburban homes of Sanderstead near to South Croydon in Surrey. Without warning a violent explosion flung from their feet men outdoors working in their gardens or "digging for victory" as the phrase of the day ran, in allotments. Floors leapt and trembled and jugs of liquid alone and untouched flung their contents over the edge as if spilt by an invisible hand. A crater appeared in Purley Oaks Road eight feet across and almost as deep, as the force of the explosion struck dead the wife of a gardener as she crossed the open grounds while her husband, although indoors suffered injuries from which he subsequently died.

The problem of some sort of defence against such as this was frequently discussed at the working lunches given by Winston Churchill at regular intervals to his Service chiefs and at one such held at Chequers in November 1944 the question came up again although there were those who thought that with its limited strategic value the capture of the launching sites was the best method of dealing with the threat. However, Churchill expressed his concern at what he regarded as some measure of improvement which had become evident in the aim. Consequently, although Anti-aircraft Command was bedevilled by manpower cuts while still stretched to provide defence against the airborne flying bomb, a scheme was devised in co-operation with a small selection of scientists by which it could be possible, at least in theory, to detonate the rockets in the air; the size of the problem may be judged when it is stated that the war-head represented only a fraction of the total length of under fifty feet so that the aim was critical even with proximity fuses in the shells. To damage the casing or flight controls would have been useless so that nothing but the complete destruction of the missile by its own explosive charge would do.

There was opposition to the scheme from some quarters who argued that the sudden firing of the guns would only cause panic if there was no warning siren, while there would be a danger to life from falling splinters almost as great as that from the explosion of the missile. Against this were those, including General Sir Frederick Pile the G.O.C.-in-C. of Anti-Aircraft Command who argued that the dangers were far outweighed by the advantages and that people enjoyed the sound of the defences "hitting back".

However that may have been, it was first necessary to detect the rocket while it was approaching its target at a speed greater than that of sound. The only way of doing this seemingly impossible task by the standards of the day was by the employment of radar and so a range of specially modified sets was deployed along the east coast in December. However it immediately became apparent that these were being expected to cope with ranges far in excess of those for which they had been designed involving altitudes in the region of ten times higher than had been planned for and at ranges almost five times greater. Throughout the month and during that following, the work continued but it soon became obvious that too much was being expected of the equipment and a new approach was indicated so that in February 1945 a series of tests began which looked more hopeful. By the middle of March it was obvious that things were on the right track at last and it became possible to predict the position of a falling rocket so that the anti-aircraft guns could place a curtain of bursting shells in its path while it was still over thirty miles from its target. But theory was one thing, practical tests were called for and an approach to the War Cabinet was made for permission to try the scheme out; this was at a time when the number of missiles falling on London had considerably diminished and before anything further could be done the attacks ceased completely when the Allied Armies overran the launching sites. Even so, the idea was a bold one to attempt to meet, in effect, tomorrow's weapons with to-day's defences and it has been suggested that the first possibilities of success were in the region of ten per cent, a figure which would certainly have been improved upon with experience.

However, these events lay in the future when the London bombardment was at its height and mindful that nothing could be done to change matters it was almost as if people began to disregard them, or at least look on them as something inevitable so that life on the surface went on very much as it had since 1939. A shattering explosion and an earth tremor would mean that somewhere rescue workers would have to begin excavations which might have to go on for three days and finally extract only bodies. Wherever you were or whatever you did there was no way of escape. Mr Keith Jackson was a solicitor and gave his spare time to such activities as chairing the Sportsmen's Appeal Committee of the local hospital; it was December 1944 and the annual Christmas Ball was to be held but Mr Jackson decided not to attend as he had a cold and his wife remained at home with him. They decided to go to bed early since there was little chance of visitors due to the bad weather. When the V-2 hurtled out of the night, Mrs Jackson and the maid were killed instantly and Mr Jackson was taken to the hospital where the sounds of the dance could still be indistinctly heard in the ward where he died from his injuries.

Another distinctive double report might make your drink leap in its glass and you wondered where that one was; Smithfield Market perhaps or it may have been the one which landed beside a train as it was pulling out of London Bridge Station, the driver was Mr Herbert Cooper and he was injured, yet he ignored his wounds to obtain assistance for his passengers, winning a commendation from the King in doing so. A typical incident was that in October when a rocket fell in the residential area of London, south of the Thames, there were six killed and forty-six wounded and quite suddenly the scene would have been changed as Army alsatians sniffed over the rubble to discover if any sign of life lay beneath and a cry for silence would go up so that the source of some feeble tapping might be more easily sought.

Unlike the flying bomb incidents there was fire on occasion when a rocket exploded. One such was at Aldgate on 10 November 1944 instantly converting the everyday scene to one of chaos; all around lay rubble several feet thick over which scrambled policemen, their helmets marking them out from the 'tin hats' of the rescue workers and firemen. Always the inevitable firemen silhouetted against the grey palls of smoke. During September they clanged through the streets to answer fifteen calls connected with rockets: in the following months, twenty-five, but the peak was reached in February 1945 when 116 V-2s came down in the London Area of the National Fire Service and there was only one fewer the following month.

A particularly spectacular incident was that at Hughes Buildings, Stepney. This was an early example of the high-rise buildings of the day and consisted of several blocks of flats fairly close together. Among these fell a V-2 which swathed out a great wasteland between two blocks. Into this fell a considerable quantity of masonry to clear which mechanical shovels had to be used and a search had to be made for the victims feared buried underneath. The smaller, surrounding houses had damage ranging from roofs totally removed to walls split at the edge of the area.

In this type of warfare, organizations such as the Royal Observer Corps were powerless and the limit of their work could be no more than the plotting of those points where rockets fell which, as accuracy of aiming improved, was increasingly inside the London area. Before this many had landed in East Anglia and even the North Sea, two facts which it is easy to glean from the post logs where all the sightings of an area were recorded. One feature of interest is that a single post logged close on 500 sightings of vapour trails and explosions although due to the extreme altitude at which many were observed it should be remembered that some duplication of sightings was inevitable; even so when it is stated that the post in question was situated in the group centred at Watford, then 17 Group, it shows that a considerable number of the rough total of 1,000 rockets which fell on this country were finally delivered into the Greater London area. More than this number were undoubtedly launched but, as with the flying bomb there were cases of failure to lift off, malfunctioning in the air or disintegration at altitude.

That there was a distinct danger of faults appearing in operational A-4s is evident when it is stated that the entire concept of a surface to surface missile was then quite new and untried so that the engineering principles were of fresh concept throughout. The Nazi rocket consisted of a cylindrical body fitted with four fins and tapered at the nose which contained the war-head. Immediately behind this was contained the equipment for the radio control and guidance beam. In the main body of the missile was the first of a pair of gigantic fuel tanks, each being almost three times the length of the explosive section, and packed in glass fibre, one of the first uses of the substance as insulation on a military project. The forward tank contained ethyl-alcohol and water while that aft

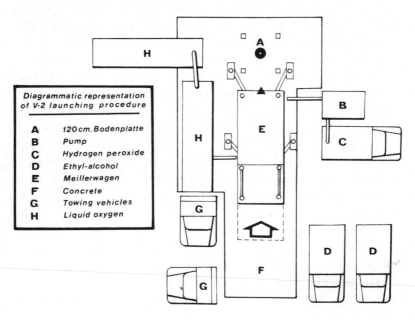

Diagrammatic representation
of V-2 launching procedure

A	120 cm. Bodenplatte
B	Pump
C	Hydrogen peroxide
D	Ethyl-alcohol
E	Meillerwagen
F	Concrete
G	Towing vehicles
H	Liquid oxygen

of it carried liquid oxygen. These two liquids were fed aft by a set of centrifugal pumps driven by steam and oxygen derived from eighty per cent hydrogen peroxide. This in turn was obtained from calcium permanganate granules decomposed catalytically after having been fed into a small gas generator from a tank by compressed nitrogen situated beside the turbo-pumps.

The ethyl-alcohol tank was pressurized with nitrogen, and the liquid oxygen depended on its own pressure to prime the pump, aft of which the fuel mixture was injected into the combustion chamber via valves such as had been introduced after the accidental destruction of A-1 on subsequent experimental models.

Entry into the chamber was not direct, but via a circulatory route due to the necessity for keeping down the temperature of the walls which were only welded up from mild steel. Consequently the alcohol and water mixture was passed round the outside of the chamber and then a part injected through small holes into the inside to cool the walls in contact with the hot gases. After this it was diverted into the main body of the combustion area to provide the thrust.

To obtain the initial thrust for launching a type of pyrotechnic rather like a 'Catherine wheel' firework was used inside to induce the first ignition of the gases which thereafter were self-firing from the residual heat.

At Christmas 1944 it was still possible to see the reflection of the V-2s as they were launched from the Continent as a climbing ball of fire in the grey sky and at the same time came news of von Rundstedt's offensive in the Ardennes and reports continued to be issued from Berlin which ran on the predictable lines that there was "heavy, harassing fire against London", echoed in such British communiqués as "Yesterday the enemy directed V-bomb fire against Southern England. Casualties and damage have been reported", which might have meant that somewhere perhaps some golfers enjoying a quiet afternoon's round in a brief respite from their war work had been slain, or that a once quiet neighbourhood was suddenly alive with a milling mass of soldiers, police, firemen and rescue workers searching a devastated area, or, and the fact must be faced, if the site of the incident was difficult to reach or the emergency services were stretched by an earlier explosion, the first arrivals might have just as easily been an organized band of looters who had been waiting with a car for a quick turn-out to the spot marked by the familiar column of smoke.

Better things were, however, just round the corner, and as spring advanced so did the armies of General Montgomery, while one column thrust across the Rhine, a second swung along the Dutch border to sever the rocket supply lines; the final V-2 hurtled to its British grave on 28 March and the citizens of southern England who had latterly shared their ordeal with those of Antwerp waited for the next fall. It never came; nine days later a Canadian armoured column advanced in eight hours some twelve miles north-east from Almelo and the final supply line to the rocket area from the assembly plants near Zutphen was cut.

The V-2 had finally been beaten by the ordinary soldier on the ground: there had been no proven defence against it and ordinary people of England and Belgium as well as Allied troops in that country had died in consequence, it was a far cry from the ideals of young Dr von Braun who had seen the publication about fifteen years before of a book entitled *Die Rakete als Weltfriedenstaube* – (The Rocket, Dove of World Peace) a sentiment evidently not shared by the young Spitfire pilot, who, returning with his formation from a sortie with 602 Squadron over northern France, with the instant reactions of a good fighting man fired a burst at a V-2 which suddenly reared out of the cloud in front of him. Perhaps due to the fact that he was more used to applying horizontal instead of vertical deflection, he missed – luckily!

Such then, was the sorry tale of man's first attempt to prostitute his knowledge of the solar system as a means of destroying his fellows. Things had come a very long way between the first record of a rocket falling on Chiswick out of the September sky at 7.43 p.m. taking the lives of three people and injuring twenty others in addition to setting alight a gas main and that which marked the final attack at 7.45 p.m. in Kynaston Road, Orpington, Kent. Between those dates the general attitude towards them had been changed considerably in this country, ranging from plans to begin a massive large-scale evacuation of London, no doubt prompted by the Nazi announcement of an anticipated 500 tons an hour delivery to a realization that what human beings can conceive, so can they deal with, and later measures against the V-2 even went into such detail as steps to ensure the closure of the London Underground System's flood-gates as from 8 January 1945 and a projected warning system signalled by firing maroons. The ambitious evacuation plans were never pursued but the threat was considered sufficiently serious for the return of persons who left during the main period of the V-1 attacks to be officially discouraged.

In addition to Operation 'Hydra' by the Royal Air Force, the United States Eighth Air Force had employed 413 Boeing B-17s to drop 958 tons of bombs over Peenemünde on 18 July and there had been another attack the following month. August had also seen attacks on other, connected targets such as that on the twenty-fourth when 128 American bombers had concentrated an assault on the radio factories at Weimar and Buchenwald while factories engaged in the production of rocket fuels in northern France and Belgium were also raided.

During the early days of the V-2 rocket attacks the British Press, although knowing full well what was going on, maintained a commendable silence reporting only those neutral sources which had immediate access to Nazi material, but it was sufficient for readers to draw their own conclusions when they read of the Swedish *Aftonbladet*'s correspondent observing after a visit to Berlin "The new secret weapon was the only topic of conversation to-day", while New Yorkers pointed out the similarity in the simultaneous flood of material from these sources and the silence from London with the attitude adopted at the immediate beginning of the V-1 attacks. The conspiracy was finally broken in November when the "Full Dramatic Story" hit the British headlines and the *Daily Mail*, in its issue for Friday the tenth presented on the front page of its late edition a remarkably accurate artist's conception by Montague Black of a V-2 being fired and with it presented a remark, picked up from a military spokesman on Berlin radio that judgement should be withheld on the effect that the new weapons was likely to have on military decisions; a reasoned opinion which was at once interpreted as representing some doubt as to the usefulness of the rocket.

The twin missiles which opened the assault in September, a second had fallen harmlessly in Pardon Woods on the same date, were launched from sites near the Hague and in the vicinity of the Scheldt estuary and all those directed against London continued to be fired from the same source until about 20 September when, after continuous attention from RAF Fighter Command coupled with harassment of the road, rail and inland waterway supply lines plus attacks on the bridges over the Ijssel River by the Second Tactical Air Force, the launching facilities were withdrawn to the Friesland area to avoid being outflanked by the advance of the Allied armies. From this new point, firings were made against Norwich which did not cease until the former sites were occupied once more while the Battle of Arnhem was in progress when London attacks were resumed.

When the last of the flying bombs and the rockets had ceased there came the time to count the cost: 8,958 dead and 24,504 injured, a total which could easily have been higher if '*Vergeltung 3*' had ever been put to use, this, a gigantic long-range gun was found lurking in a huge underground emplacement in the Mimoyecques district of the Pas de Calais. One of many, it was capable of firing rocket shells against London but frequent pounding of the RAF's Bomber Command had prevented it becoming more than a hideous dream, as it was 1,368 V-1s and 3,002 V-2s were found by the victorious Allies which scheduled the whole collection to be destroyed by the Air Disarmament Wings in the now largely forgotten but aptly named Operation 'Eclipse'.

Appendix I
General Specifications

V-1 (FZG 76)
Span: 5.3m (17ft 4½in.); *length:* 7.7m (25ft 4½in.) – United States Intelligence reports described a tapered wing version of 4.87m (16ft) span with a maximum cord of 1.04m (41in.) tapering to .81m (2ft 8in.) at the tip; *fuselage diameter:* .838m (2ft 9in.); *engine diameter:* .58m (1ft 10¾in.); *operational weight:* 2,180kg (4,796lb); *explosive weight:* (850kg (1,870lb), later reduced to 454kg (1,000lb); *motor:* Argus As 109-014 Rohr delivering 350kg (770lb) thrust at sea level; *maximum speed:* 654km/hr (400 m.p.h.); *ceiling:* 3,000m (8,840ft).

Reichenberg III (R-111)
Span: 5.3m (17ft 4½in.); *length:* 8.5m (27ft 9in.); (Reichenberg IV: 8m (26ft 3in.); *fuselage diameter:* .838m (2ft 9in.); *engine diameter:* .58m (1ft 10¾in.); *motor:* Argus As 109-014 Rohr delivering 350kg (770lb) thrust at sea level; *maximum speed:* 645km/hr (400 m.p.h.).

V-2
Span: 3.6m (11ft 8½in.); *length:* 14.4m (46ft 11in.); *body diameter:* 1.6m (5ft 5in.); *operational weight:* 12,805kg (28,229lb); *explosive weight:* 998kg (2,200lb); *maximum speed:* 6,080km/hr (3,800 m.p.h.); *range:* 304km (190m.).

Ford JB-2
Span: 17ft 8in. (5.4m); *length:* 27ft 1in. (8.3m); *operational weight:* 5,025lb (2,279kg); *explosive weight:* 2,000lb (907kg); *motor:* Ford IJ-15-1; *maximum speed:* 440 m.p.h. (704km/hr); *ceiling:* 6,000ft (2,000m).

Appendix 2
Colour Schemes

V-1 (FZG 76)

When the unmanned flying bomb was first used over southern England reports which have remained unconfirmed described them as being finished dark brown or black. One of those preserved at RAF Henlow is doped entirely in the latter shade but it is not known if this is an original scheme. Certainly it was not long before they were camouflaged in black-green (70 *Schwarzgrün* 30F8) on the upper surfaces and light blue (65 *Hellblau* 24A4) over the lower areas. The entire jet unit was regarded as an upper surface and doped to suit. On the fuselage the division between the colours took place along an undulating line from tail to nose which usually passed over the wing surface. This line frequently failed to match up on adjacent sections and the metal cone supporting the air log and forming the nose section was almost always doped all over in the upper surface green, while the fin and rudder were regarded as lower surfaces and doped accordingly.

There were some variations: wooden war-heads could be finished yellow (04 *Gelb* 4A8) all over. This is thought to be derived from the system of bomb identification and would indicate SC (*Sprengbombe Cylindrisch*), a thin-walled, general purpose, high explosive bomb; while there were those which had a coat of distemper on the lower surfaces of the wings and tailplane of very pale yellow. Applied over the light-blue colour the resultant shade was a pale green-yellow. (2B5-6). Some wings only were doped in a splinter camouflage (see Reichenberg details) and used in conjunction with the black-green/light blue scheme. Wing leading edge demarcation could take the form of an undulating line set back on the upper surface about ten centimetres, others were straight along the front.

At least from the first week in August, flying bombs were being launched with the metal surfaces entirely bare.

Stencilled instructions were marked in black or black-green on the

166

light finish and in light blue on the dark. The only exception to this was *'Klebestreifen auf Unterseite-Inbestriebnahme entfernen'* on the port side which was in red (23 *Rot* 10B8). Characters were of three heights; 34 mm, 15 mm and 8 mm.

Air-launched bombs were finished during the early trials in light grey (76 *Hellgrau* (22-23)A2) above and black below. A number was stencilled on the upper part of the fin. The Heinkels acting as parent machines were doped in a splinter scheme on top and sides of black-green and dark green (71 *Dunkelgrün* (29-30)F3). Operational missiles were finished no differently from the catapult-launched versions except that a greater number of the former had an irregular dividing line running down the mid-line of the jet unit, the lower part of which was doped light blue. Heinkel 111s used as carriers were, for the most part, camouflaged above and in some cases on the sides, in an overall scheme of light grey, covered with irregular patches of dark grey (74 *Dunkelgrau* 21(E-F)3). Underparts were entirely black, and this was occasionally extended roughly over the fuselage sides between the rear of the wing and tailplane leading edge. Sometimes the code on the side was reduced to no more than the single individual machine identification in the Staffel colour.

Reichenberg

The piloted missiles were camouflaged similarly to some single-seat fighters at the same time, namely an undersurface shade of light grey merging into a mottled and smudged form of splinter pattern of dark grey and middle grey (75 *Mittlegrau* 23D(2-3)). The demarcation line was hardly discernible but the patches of colour tended to be larger and more pronounced down to a point at about a ten degree tangent below the centre line on both motor unit and fuselage and sometimes well below this point towards the rear and on the engine pipe where it met the lower colour in a 'soft' undulating line. Unlike the FZG 76, vertical tail surfaces were treated as upper parts and doped accordingly. Cockpit interiors were finished in the so-called RLM Grey (02 RLM *Grau* 1(C-D)4).

No national markings of any type were carried at any time on either the FZG 76 or the Reichenbergs, although some photographs do exist showing, on a few captured examples of the latter, rudder swastikas, perhaps a last minute addition in case they were pressed into service.

Some Reichenberg missiles were doped on top and sides in a

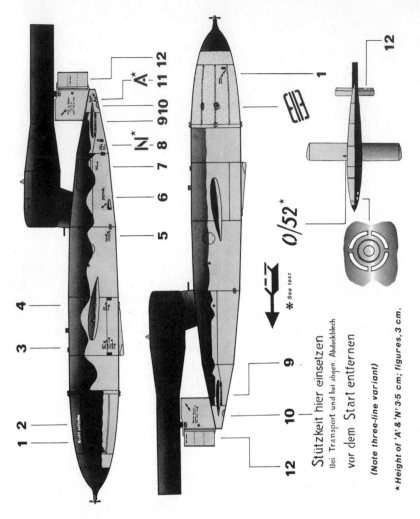

Application of camouflage colours to FZG 76 and position of stencilled instructions

	Key	Height in centimetres	Colour if not black-green.
1	Abstellpallung **N**		
	Herkules	* 2	Light blue on some.
2	Nicht auftreten (Both sides alike)	4	Light blue
3	Waggon		
	Kfz		
	TW76 **N**		

MT12 **N**

Rollpallung **N**
LWC
Abstellpallung **A**
Doppelpallung   2
4 MT12
LWC
Rollpallung Kurz

TW76 **A**

5 TW76A **N**   2
Rollpallunglang
Zubringerwagen (Schlitten) * (some)   2
6 Klebestreifen auf Unterseitevor
Inbetriebnahme entfernen   *   1   Red
7 TW76A
Doppelpallung   2
8 Kfz Verladung
(Pallungsabstand b2)

Herkules N **N**
Abstellpallung N   2
9 Abstellbock   *   2
10 Stützkeit hier einsetzen   *   2
Bei Transport und bui abgen.   1
Abdeckblech   1
vor dem Start entfernen   2
11 Abstellpallung A

Herkules A **A**   2

12 Nicht anfassen   4   Light blue
above both
elevators

Heights are for upper case letters, lower case letters were 5 mm less
in height except for the 4 cm characters which should be reduced by
1 cm for the lower case stencilling.
* Indicates an arrow, 9 cm long beside the instruction, the style and
direction of which may be found on the drawing. Note that
instruction 9 incorporates two, before and after the word, the first
pointing towards the leading edge, the second, aft.

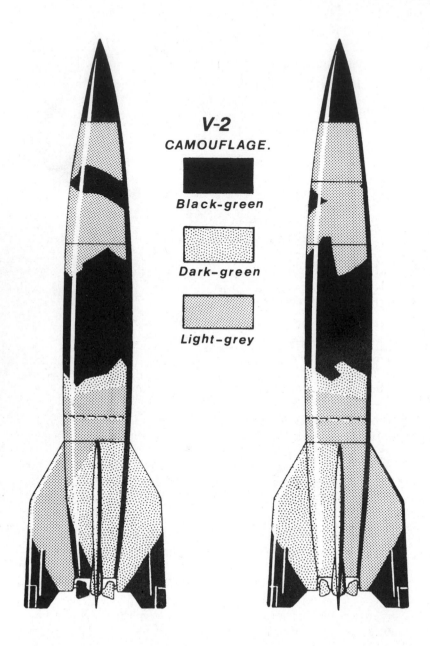

V-2
CAMOUFLAGE.

Black-green

Dark–green

Light–grey

'Wave Mirroe' pattern of dark green and light blue, which colour was also employed for the underparts.

V-2

A-4 rockets were sprayed over their entire surface with a coat of black-green, but a lesser number were finished in a broad splinter camouflage pattern of this shade combined with dark green and light grey. Those employed for test work were for the most part finished in various combinations of black and white in a geometrical pattern to assist observation.

Ford JB-2 ('Loon')

Standard finish for American flying bombs was a coat of olive drab, U.S. Ref.41ANA613 (30F6), over both upper and lower surfaces. However, entirely white wings, both above and below were common, as were white war-heads, excluding the streamlined nose cone, which were often hastily overpainted thus just before launching. If war-heads remained olive drab, they were often daubed with a large and crudely-applied two-digit numeral in white.

Ford JB-2s alone among the missiles described, carried national markings which consisted of the familiar white star of the period against a blue, U.S. Ref. 47ANA605 (21(E-F)8), disc which had white rectangles at each side, these in turn being edged in the same shade of blue. Markings were applied to each side of the fuselage with their forward extremity in line with the leading edge of the pulse-jet, and above the port wing and below the starboard.

Similar insignia was carried by the later 'Loon' variant but the colour schemes of these robots may be described as entirely white, relieved only by olive drab dope on the war-head, rudder, that section of the fuselage bearing the markings and jet unit, although it was not extended here to the faired, front mounting fork. These white areas were intended as a photographic aid, while those which survived into the 1950s were doped red and yellow with black fin numerals.

Footnote: The two-digit combinations quoted for the Nazi weapons is the *Luftwaffe* code and shade description as laid down in *Farbtonkerte nach* (Colour Standards) LDv 521/2, November 194ſ. The letter/number combinations throughout indicates the colour notation under the Methuen system of shade definition.

Appendix 3
Location of Preserved V-1 and Associated Missiles

V-1 (FZG 76)

Australia
Australian War Memorial, Canberra

Canada
National Aeronautical Collection, Rockliffe

Denmark
Royal Danish Arsenal Museum, Copenhagen

Great Britain
Ian Stone's Restaurant, Pickering, North Yorkshire
Imperial War Museum, Lambeth, London. (Werk Nr 477663)
Ministry of Technology Rocket Propulsion Establishment, Westcott, Buckinghamshire. (Werk Nr 418947)
Cosford Aero-Space Museum, Wolverhampton, Staffordshire. (Two Specimens)
Royal Engineers, Rochester (Fort Clarence) Kent*
Science Museum, South Kensington, London. (Werk Nr 442795)

Netherlands
War Museum, Overloon

New Zealand
Domain War Memorial Museum, Auckland

Sweden
Technical Museum, Stockholm

*A conventional FZG 76 modified to represent a Reichenberg IV.

United States of America
Elemdorf Air Force base, Alaska
Morgan's Lumber Yard, Morgan, Nevada
Air Force Space Museum, Patrick AF Base, Cape Kennedy, Florida
Planes of Fame Museum, Buena Park, California
Roswell Museum Missile Collection, Rosewell, New Mexico
U.S. Army Ordnance Centre and School Museum, Aberdeen, Maryland

REPLICA V-1
Great Britain
Shuttleworth Trust Collection, Old Warden, Bedfordshire

REICHENBERG IV
Netherlands
Technical University, Leiden

FORD JB-2
United States of America
Aerospace Park, Hampton, Virginia
Alabama Space & Rocket Centre, Alabama
Dayton Air Force Museum, Dayton, Ohio (two missiles)
Holloman Air Force Base, New Mexico
Lackland Air Force Base, New Mexico
North Island NAS, San Diego, California
Travel Town Museum, Griffith Park, California
U.S. Marine Corps Museum, Quantico, Virginia

Appendix 4
Facts and Figures

V-1

Number of bombs to approach coast:	6,725
Casualties (approx.);	
Killed:	5,500
Injured:	18,000
Houses destroyed:	23,000
Number launched in first twenty-four hours:	155
Number launched on worst day (2 August):	316
Approximate cost:	£120
Number destroyed	
by anti-aircraft guns:	1,859
by fighters:	1,846
by balloons (approx.):	230
Maximum number destroyed by guns in single day:	68
Successful night interceptions by fighters:	142
Maximum number of anti-aircraft guns deployed; (3.7in.):	542
(40mm):	503
Number of guns deployed in Diver Box;	
(3.7in.):	136
(40mm):	210
(20mm):	410
First bomb to cross coast:	13 June 1944
Last bomb to cross coast:	29 March 1945
Number of public air-raid warnings sounded:	402

V-2

Number of rockets fired successfully:	1,178
Number to reach London area:	517
Number to fall on other parts of Great Britain:	537
Number to fall into North Sea:	58
Number to burst in the air over London:	60

Appendix 6
Incorporation of V-1 Ramps into the Countryside

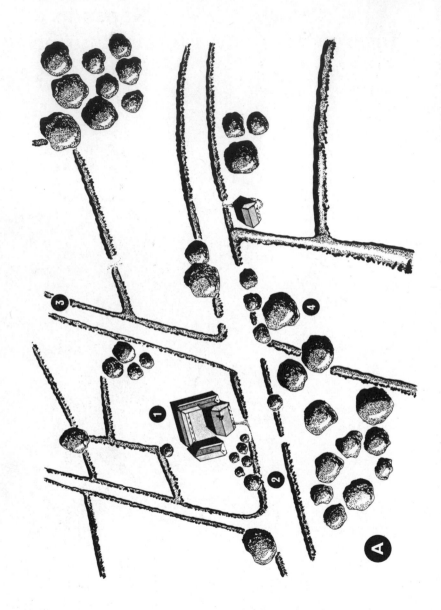

A. Countryside before the erection of a flying-bomb site.
Key: 1, farm buildings; 2, public road; 3, lane; 4, wood

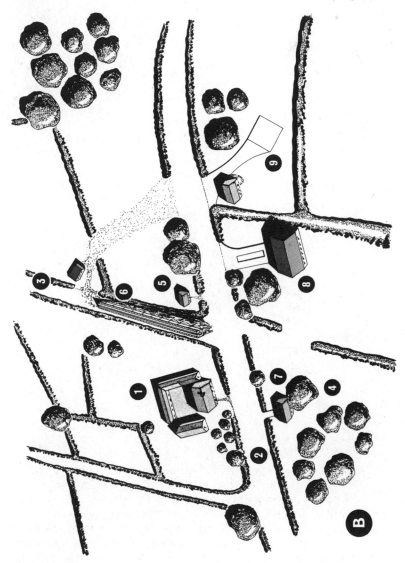

B. The same area after erection of a flying-bomb ramp to make use of natural features of the area. **Key:** 1, farm buildings; 2, public road; 3, lane; 4, wood, partially cut down in direction of launch; 5, fire point; 6, launching ramp; 7, fuel dump; 8, assembly building; 9, non-magnetic area for swinging compass

Internal Details of a Type 1 Flying Bomb

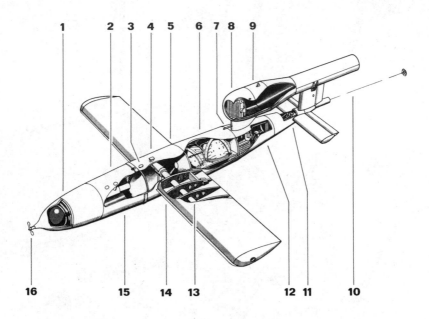

Internal details of a Type 1 flying bomb. **Key**: 1, compass to control gyros for guidance, enclosed in non-magnetic (wooden) sphere; 2, twin fuse pockets in horizontal main fuse; 3, fuel filler cap; 4, lifting lug; 5, fuel tank; 6, wire-bound compressed air spheres for pneumatic control motors; 7, ram tube; 8, jet motor flanked by mixing venturis; 9, combustion chamber; 10, 400-foot aerial for ranging transmitter; 11, pneumatic motors to operate controls; 12, battery, fuel and guidance controls; 13, wooden ribs (some were metal) on tubular metal spar; 14, cable cutter (optional, one of two forms); 15, war-head; 16, air log to determine length of flight

* Early, experimental air-launched bombs had an external, unfaired front fork mounting for the pulse jet

Appendix 8
Location of Preserved V-2 Rockets

Australia
Australian Army Headquarters, Holsworth
Australian War Memorial, Canberra

Germany
Luftwaffen Museum, Uetersen

Great Britain
Imperial War Museum, Lambeth, London
Ministry of Technology Rocket Propulsion Establishment, Westcott, Buckinghamshire
RAF Henlow, Bedfordshire

United States of America
Alabama Space and Rocket Centre, Alabama
Dayton Air Force Museum, Dayton, Ohio
National Air and Space Museum, Washington DC
Roswell Museum Missile Collection, Roswell, New Mexico
U.S. Army Ordnance Centre and School Museum, Aberdeen, Maryland

Appendix 9
Three-view drawings of V-1 and Reichenberg Missiles

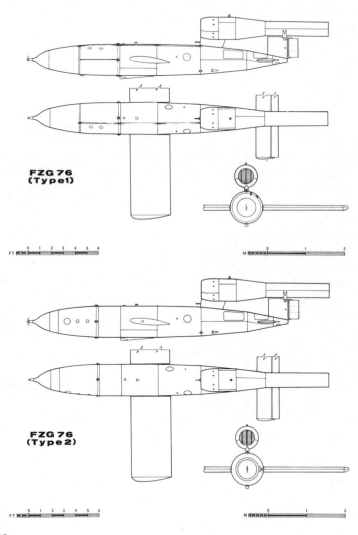

FZG 76
(Type1)

FT 0 1 2 3 4 5 6

M 0 1 2

FZG 76
(Type2)

FT 0 1 2 3 4 5 6

M 0 1 2

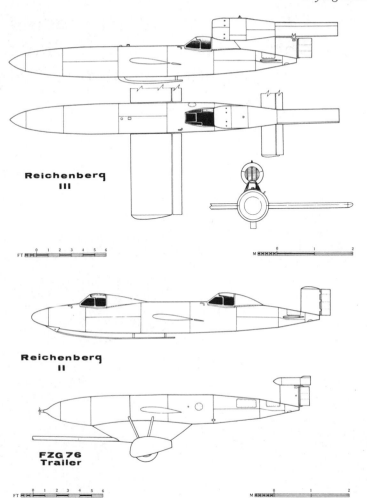

Reichenberg III

Reichenberg II

FZG 76 Trailer

Appendix 10
V-2 Bases and Connected Railheads in France, September 1944

Storage Depot	Railhead
Agenville	Aux le Château
Auchy-les-Hesdin	Auchy-les-Hesdin
Bergueneuse	Anvin
La Pourchinte	Lumbers
Lumbers	Lumbers
Pont Remy	Pont Remy
Raimbert	Raimbert or Calonne Ricort and Lapugnoy
Rollencourt	Blangy sur Ternoise
St Ricquier	St Ricquier

Appendix 11
V-Weapon Casualties in Europe
1944-45

	Antwerp	Brussels	Liège	Remagen	Others	Totals
Military Killed	743	7	92	3	111	947
Military Wounded	1,078	38	336	15	442	1,909
Total	1,812	45	428	18	553	2,856
Civilians Killed	2,900	40	221	0	575	3,736
Civilians Injured	5,433	153	937	0	1,643	8,166
Total	8,333	193	1,158	0	2,218	11,902
Grand Total	10,145	238	1,586	18	2,771	14,758

Other Continental Centres Bombarded

Arras	Maastricht
Cambrai	Mons
Diest	Paris
Hasselt	Tourcoign
Lille	Tournai

Appendix 12
Representative Fighter Squadron Scores. V-1

No.	Type	Base	Score
3	Tempest 5	New Church/ Matlask	257½
486	Tempest 5	New Church	223½
91	Spitfire 14	Deanland	185
96*	Mosquito 13	Ford	174
322	Spitfire 14	West Malling/ Deanland	108½
418*	Mosquito 6	Holmesby Sth/ Hurn/Middle Wallop	90
129	Mustang 3	Brenzett	66

*Night fighter squadrons.
N.B. The system of allocating victory confirmations was that a flying bomb shot down over the sea counted as one enemy aircraft destroyed, while one brought down on land was rated as equal to one half.

Appendix 13
Representative Fighter Patrols Against Air-Launched Flying Bombs, March 1945

Date	Bombs Launched	To Land	To London	Destroyed by Day	Night	A.A.	Sorties Day	Night	RN
1	—	—	—	—	—	—	—	15	—
2	13	1	1	—	—	6	—	25	—
3	9	4	1	—	—	4	19	27	—
4	3	3	1	—	—	—	19	—	—
5	10	5	4	—	—	2	26	—	—
6	8	4	—	1	—	3	18	13	—
7	—	—	—	—	—	—	22	1	—
8	3	1	—	—	—	2½	19	13	½
9	—	—	—	—	—	—	16	—	—
10	—	—	—	—	—	—	14	—	—
11	—	—	—	—	—	—	17	—	—
12	—	—	—	—	—	—	10	—	—
13	—	—	—	—	—	—	16	—	—
14	6	1	1	—	—	5	10	1	—
15	4	3	—	—	—	3	8	2	—
16	1	—	—	—	—	—	11	—	—
17	5	1	—	—	—	4	16	4	—
18	2	—	—	—	—	1	15	5	—
19	9	4	—	—	—	1	11	4	—
20	2	—	—	—	—	2	17	2	—
21	3	2	—	—	—	3	16	4	—
22	12	1	—	—	—	10	12	6	—
23	6	3	—	—	—	1	20	—	—
24	3	3	1	1	—	—	18	—	—
25	14	7	1	1	—	7	14	—	—

Flying Bomb

Date	Bombs			Destroyed by			Sorties		
	Launched	To Land	To London	Day	Night	A.A.	Day	Night	RN
26	9	5	1	—	1	4	—	8	—
27	10	2	—	—	—	9	17	4	—
28	15	5	2	—	—	12	—	1	1
29	12	5	—	—	—	8	15	—	—
30	—	—	—	—	—	—	16	—	—
31	—	—	—	—	—	—	14	—	—
Totals	159	60	13	3	1	87½	426	135	1½

Appendix 14
Representative Attacks on V-2 and Associated Targets, November 1944-April 1945

2nd TAF

	Aircraft	Tons Dropped	Target
November			
2	12 Typhoons	—	Leeuwarden area
	16 Spitfires	2	Rosendall
4	12 Typhoons	—	Leeuwarden area
6	8 Typhoons	—	Amersfoort/Zwolle
	10 Typhoons	—	Apeldoorn/Amersfoort
	16 Typhoons	7	Arnhem area
	8 Typhoons	4	Deventer area
	8 Typhoons	4	Zutphen area
December			
5	8 Typhoons	—	Venlo area
11	32 Typhoons	17	Leiden
	(One aircraft failed to return)		
12	35 Mosquitos	1	Leiden
	(The larger percentage consisted of fighters)		
17	35 Mosquitos	1	Leiden
	(Sortie composition as previous attack)		
29	8 Typhoons	1	Osnabruck area
?	35 Spitfires	7	Zwolle/Hilversum
January 1945			
14	31 Typhoons	13	Hellendoorn area
	(One aircraft failed to return)		
	35 Spitfires	16	Hellendoorn area
20/22	16 Typhoons	—	Unknown
	118 Spitfires	21	Alblasserdam
	(One aircraft failed to return)		

	Aircraft	Tons Dropped	Target
February			
3/6	47 Spitfires	13	Nijverdal
	35 Spitfires	7	Apeldoorn area
6	12 Spitfires	3	Hellendoorn
21	18 Typhoons	4	Heek
	(One aircraft failed to return)		
	8 Typhoons	3	Zeist
	(Some aircraft armed with rocket projectiles used on both of the above raids)		
25	73 Mosquitos	44	Holten, Marienburg and Xanten
March			
3	16 Spitfires	5	Zwolle
	17 Bostons	10	Haagsche Bosch/Hague
	44 Mitchells	77	Haagsche Bosch/Hague
13	11 Typhoons	3	Raalte
19	11 Spitfires	5	Raalte
23	17 Typhoons	3	Rotterdam area
	FIGHTER COMMAND		
1	45 Spitfires	11	Haagsche Bosche
	(Sortie flown in bad weather, 33 aircraft failed to find target)		
	10 Spitfires	2	Gouda Railway Junction
2	46 Spitfires	13	Haagsche Bosch
	(Fighter-bombers accompanied by 20 fighters)		
	11 Spitfires	5	Wassenaar/Rust
	12 Spitfires	5	Staalduine Bosch
3	52 Spitfires	14	Haagsche Bosch
	16 Spitfires	4	Wassenaar/Rust
	4 Spitfires	1	Staalduine Bosch
	(Fighter-bombers accompanied by 4 fighters)		
	7 Spitfires	2	Ockenburg
	11 Spitfires	2	Gouda and Alphen Junctions
4	13 Spitfires	4	Wassenaar/Rust
	8 Spitfires	4	Ockenburg
	(Sortie flown in heavy cloud, 7 aircraft failed to find target.)		

	Aircraft	Tons Dropped	Target
	Fighter-bombers accompanied by 4 fighters)		
	4 Spitfires	1	Bataasche factories
	8 Spitfires	—	Staalduine Bosch
	(No bombs dropped due to bad weather)		
	8 Spitfires	2	Hague area railways
	4 Spitfires	1	A.S. Rocket defences Hague
5	8 Spitfires	2	Hague Racecourse
	(Fighter-bombers accompanied by 3 fighters)		
	7 Spitfires	2	Wassendaar/Rust
	(Fighter-bombers accompanied by 4 fighters)		
	12 Spitfires	3	Duindigt Racecourse
	(20 more machines failed to make attack due to deteriorating weather)		
	4 Spitfires	1	Ockenburg
	8 Spitfires	—	Staalduine Bosch
	(No bombs dropped due to cloud over target)		
	12 Spitfires	3	Hague area railways
6	8 Spitfires	—	Wassendaar/Rust
	(Raiders recalled due to bad weather)		
7	4 Spitfires	—	The Hague
	(Raiders recalled due to bad weather)		
8	6 Spitfires	—	Wassendaar/Rust
	(No bombs dropped due to cloud over target)		
	4 Spitfires	—	Duindigt Racecourse
	(No bombs dropped due to cloud over target)		
9	24 Spitfires	8	Duindigt Racecourse
	(Fighter-bombers accompanied by 8 fighters, one of which failed to return)		
	19 Spitfires	9	Wassendaar/Rust
	32 Spitfires	13	Wassendaar/Ravelijn
	19 Spitfires	4	Hague area railways
	(One aircraft failed to return)		
10	27 Spitfires	6	Duindigt Racecourse
	5 Spitfires	1	Wassendaar/Ravelijn
	(Fighter-bombers accompanied by 8 fighters. Cloud obscured target)		

	Aircraft	Tons Dropped	Target
	32 Spitfires	12	Hague railway area
	(Fighter-bombers accompanied by 8 fighters)		
11	16 Spitfires	—	Wassendaar/Ravelijn
	(Fighter-bombers accompanied by 35 fighters which shot up the area. No bombs dropped due to low cloud)		
12	7 Spitfires	1	Wassendaar/Ravelijn
	(Fighter-bombers accompanied by 3 fighters)		
	21 Spitfires	5	Duindigt Racecourse
	5 Spitfires	1	Hague railway area
	(Fighter-bombers accompanied by 4 fighters)		
13	118 Spitfires	46	Duindigt Racecourse
	16 Spitfires	—	Wassendaar/Ravelijn
14	69 Spitfires	15	Duindigt Racecourse
	14 Spitfires	3	Wassendaar/Ravelijn
	4 Spitfires	1	Hague railway area
15	3 Spitfires	1	Wassendaar/Ravelijn
	4 Spitfires	—	Duindigt Racecourse
	(No bombs dropped due to bad weather over target. Fighter-bombers accompanied by 8 fighters)		
	6 Spitfires	—	Hague/Bataasche
	(No bombs dropped due to bad weather over target)		
	8 Spitfires	2	Hague railway area
	4 Spitfires	1	Hague/Amsterdam Road
	(Bombs did not explode)		
17	148 Spitfires	51	Hague railway area
	(Fighter-bombers accompanied by 4 fighters, one of which failed to return)		
18	111 Spitfires	33	Hague railway area
	(One aircraft failed to return)		
	27 Spitfires	11	Duindigt Racecourse
	(Fighter-bombers accompanied by 4 fighters)		
	6 Spitfires	3	Bataasche factories
19	29 Spitfires	9	Hague railway area
	(Fighter-bombers accompanied by 8 fighters)		
20	125 Spitfires	50	Hague railway area
	(One aircraft failed to return)		

	Aircraft	Tons Dropped	Target
	32 Spitfires	13	Yaenburg Airfield
	2 Spitfires	—	Den Helder/ Amsterdam area
21	116 Spitfires	45	Hague railway area
22	68 Spitfires	23	Hague railway area
	52 Spitfires	22	Kurhaus Garage store
23	102 Spitfires	40	Hague roads and rail areas

(Fighter-bombers accompanied by 4 fighters)

	24 Spitfires	11	Wenburg Airfield
24	110 Spitfires	41	Hague railway area
25	102 Spitfires	39	Hague railway area

(Fighter-bombers, one of which failed to return accompanied by 4 fighters)

27	83 Spitfires	19	Hague railway area

(Fighter-bombers accompanied by 11 fighters)

30	128 Spitfires	48	Hague railway area

(Fighter-bombers accompanied by 2 fighters)

31	93 Spitfires	23	Hague railway area

April

1	4 Spitfires	—	Dutch rail targets

(No bombs dropped due to cloud over target)

2	52 Spitfires	12	Hague railway area
3	24 Spitfires	5	Hague railway area

(Fighter-bombers accompanied by 2 fighters.
Four of the fighter-bombers did not attack the target after
it became obscured by cloud)

N.B. Fighters operating alone to shoot up a target are included in the general list and are indicated by no entry in the 'Tons Dropped' column unless this is not recorded because the attack was withdrawn due to weather etc. Fighters which operated in support of a fighter-bomber sortie are noted in brackets below the listing of the bombing raid.

Appendix 15
Defence Communications

Gun Operations Room, October, 1944

1	Yarmouth	6	Thorpe
2	Theberton	7	Burnham
3	Saxmundham	8	Vange
4	Orford	9	Southend
5	Harwich	10	Chatham

Additions, February, 1945

RAF Sector Operations Rooms
Church Fenton
Digby

A.A. Gun Operations Rooms
Bridlington
Humber
Louth

Forward Control Points
(*CHL*)
Bempton
Goldsborough
Dimlington
(*GCI*)
Patrington
Orby

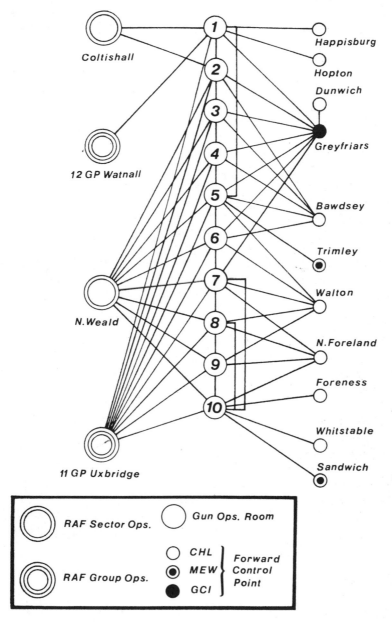

Anti-'Diver' communications system

Glossary

ABC – The ABC Aero Engine Company. Manufacturers of Walton-on-Thames, Surrey

Abstellknopf – The red button in the '*Zählwerk*' of a Heinkel bomber adapted to carry a V-1 by means of which the motor of the missile could be stopped in an emergency

AFDU – Air Fighting Development Unit

Anstellknopf – The black button in the '*Zählwerk*' of a Heinkel bomber adapted to carry a V-1 by means of which the motor of the missile was started, prior to launching

ARWO – Air Raid Warning Officer

'**Bodyline**' – General code name employed by the Allies for investigation into V-weapons

'**Big Ben**' – Allied code name for defence measures against V-2 rockets

CHL – Chain Home, Low. A type of ground-based, defence radar

'**Crossbow**' – Allied code name for defence measures against V-1 flying bombs

DFS – Deutsche Forschungsinstitut für Segelflug. Literally the German Research Institute for Sailflying

Dihedral – The angle between the wings of an aeroplane and the horizontal when viewed from the front. This effects the lateral stability of a flying machine

Erprobungskommando – Testing Command

'**Fickle**' – Allied code name for very clear weather conditions allowing fighter aircraft full freedom of action

'**Firework**' – Allied priority codeword employed to announce the actual discharge of a V-2 rocket

'**Flabby**' – Allied code name for medium weather conditions when fighters were allowed to chase flying bombs over the gun-belt to the balloon line

FuGe 101 – A type of radio altimeter in use by the Nazi *Luftwaffe*

Fuhrungsstab (der Luftwaffe) – Nazi Transport and Communications Unit of the Air Force

GCI – Ground Controlled Interception. A method of guiding Allied intercepting fighters to the vicinity of a raider.

G-H – British blind-bombing radar system employing a pair of ground transmitters to act as beacons and an airborne transmitter/receiver normally used as a navigational radio aid of about 300 miles (480 kilometres) range. Sometimes written as GeH

Hydrogen Peroxide (Nazi code named '*T-stoff*') – A colourless liquid oxidizing agent produced from catalytically decomposed calcium permanganate granules employed to drive the centrifugal steam pumps of a V-2 rocket. Also used to propel the launching piston of a V-1 Walter catapult.

'**Hydra**' (**Operation**) – Allied code name for the attack by 590 aircraft of RAF Bomber Command on the experimental station at Peenemünde during the night of 17 August 1943

Liquid Oxygen (Nazi code named '*A-stoff*') – One of the two substances used to propel the rocket motor of a V-2 missile

'**Loon**' – American code name for JB-2; copy of Nazi V-1 missile

Meillerwagen – Long Road Trailer. A type of low-loader for the transportation of V-2 rockets by road. It incorporated an elevating gear capable of lifting the missile from the horizontal to the vertical position in preparation for firing. Towing vehicle was a Hanomag SS-100

Methyl Alcohol (Nazi code named '*C-stoff*') – A mixture of 30% hydrazine hydrate, 57% methyl alcohol and 13% water. The second of the two substances used to propel the rocket motor of a V-2 missile

MEW – Microwave Early Warning

197

Mittelwerke – Central Works

'**No-ball**' – Allied code name for V-weapon sites consisting of launching areas, stores and assembly centres

'**Oboe**' – Allied code name for a system of target marking and blind bombing by means of radar. Two ground radar stations were employed, one to indicate the track and the other the target

'**Overlord**' **(Operation)** – Code name for the Allied invasion of the continent of Europe which began on 6 July 1944

Petrol (Nazi code name '*B-stoff*') – Aviation spirit for reciprocating internal combustion engines

'**Popgun**' – Allied priority codeword employed to announce the discharge of a V-2 missile observed by flash recording

PRU – Photographic Reconnaissance Unit (of the RAF)

RAE – Royal Aircraft Establishment, Farnborough, Hampshire

'**Red Fire**' **(Red Spot Fire)** – Allied name for a target marker bomb first used operationally on Operation 'Hydra'. It ignited on bursting at 3,000 feet and continued to burn on the ground for about ten minutes.

RLM – Reichsluftfahrtministerium, German Air Ministry

RN – Royal Navy

'**Rumpelkammer**' **(Operation)** – Nazi code name for the attacks on Great Britain by V-1 flying bombs which began on 13 June 1944

Selbstopfermanner – Suicide men. Pilots of 'Reichenberg' piloted flying bombs

'**Snowflake**' – Illuminating rocket flares fired by ROC posts to attract attention of fighter pilots to flying bombs

'**Spouse**' – Allied code name for bad weather when guns had complete freedom of action up to 8,000 feet altitude and fighters were required to keep above this height

Staffelkapitän – A *Hauptmann* or Captain normally in charge of a *Staffel* or Flight of the *Luftwaffe*

SS – Schutzstaffeln, sometimes written 'Schutz Staffeln', part of the Nazi armed forces; originally conceived as Hitler's personal bodyguard. Its leader was the notorious Heinrich Himmler

'**Totter**' (**Operation**) – Allied code name for the use of 'Snowflake' rockets to indicate the presence of flying bombs to fighters

Vergeltung – Revenge Weapon, Nazi propaganda name for several weapons of unconventional type

VfR – Raketenflugplatz, a German rocket research institute

Zählwerk – Term used by crews of Heinkel bombers adapted to carry V-1s, for the control box used to air-launch the missiles

Züge – Platoon

Bibliography

BABINGTON SMITH, CONSTANCE *Evidence in Camera* (Chatto and Windus, 1958 and David and Charles, 1974)

BUSHBY, JOHN R. *Air Defence of Great Britain* (Ian Allan, 1973)

CLOSTERMANN, PIERRE *The Big Show* (Chatto and Windus, 1951)

COLLIER, BASIL *A History of Air Power* (Weidenfeld & Nicholson, 1974)

DORNBERGER, GENERAL WALTHER *V-2* (Hurst and Blackett, 1954)

GARTLAND, KENNETH *Missiles and Rockets* (Blandford, 1975)

ILLINGWORTH, FRANK *Flying Bomb* (The Citizen Press, 1945)

IRVING, DAVID *The Mare's Nest* (William Kimber, 1964)

JACKSON, ERIC W. *London's Fire Brigades* (Longman, 1966)

KAY, A.L. and SMITH, J. RICHARD *German Aircraft of the Second World War* (Putnam, 1972)

LEE, WING COMMANDER ASHER *Blitz on Britain* (Four Square Books, 1960)

MOYES, PHILIP J.R. *Bomber Squadrons of the Royal Air Force* (Macdonald, 1964)

MONTAGUE, EWEN *Beyond Top Secret* (Peter Davies, 1977)

NEWMAN BERNARD *Spy and Counter-Spy* (Robert Hale, 1970)

NEWMAN, BERNARD *They Saved London* (Werner Laurie, 1952 and Panther Books, 1957)

PILE, GENERAL SIR FREDERICK *Ack-Ack* (George Harrap, 1949 and Panther Books, 1956)

POCOCK, ROWLAND F. *German Guided Missiles* (Ian Allan, 1967)

RAWLINGS, JOHN *Fighter Squadrons of the Royal Air Force* (Macdonald, 1969)

RICHARDSON W. and SEYMORE F. (Eds) *The Fatal Decisions* (Michael Joseph, 1956 and Ace Books, 1959)

SHARP, MARTIN C. and BOWYER, MICHAEL J.F. *Mosquito* (Faber, 1971)

THETFORD, OWEN G. *Aircraft of the Royal Air Force since 1918* (Putnam, 1958)

WHITTY, OBSERVER COMMANDER H. RAMSDEN (Ed) *Observers' Tale* (Privately published by Number 17 Group, Royal Observer Corps, Watford, 1950)

WILTON, ERIC *Centre Crew* (Privately published for Members of 'B' Crew, Royal Observer Corps Centre, Bromley, Kent, 1946)

Index

Index

Police, 159
Poling (Sussex), 56
Poole, Captain, 17
Portslade, 81
Portsmouth, 56, 81

Radar, 115, 117, 121
Radio programmes, 22
Radio transmitters, 39
Random Harvest, 76
Reichsluftfahrtministerium
 (RLM), 23-5
Reitsch, Flugkapitän Hanna,
 26, 133
Ringstead, 56
Rogers, Flying Officer, 105
Rose Marie, 75
Royal Aircraft Establishment,
 16-7, 98
Royal Air Force:
 Groups:
 No.10, 56
 No.11, 57, 102
 No.12, 58-9
 Wings:
 No.125, 49
 Squadrons:
 No.3, 59
 No.26, 59
 No.56, 59
 No.80, 59
 No.84, 18
 No.132, 46, 48-9
 No.140, 59
 No.229, 59
 No.274, 59
 No.322, 104
 No.540, 59
 No.544, 59
 No.602, 46, 48-9
 No.605, 58
 No.616, 104-5
 Stations:
 Benson PRU, 42, 54, 57

Coltishall, 59
Danesfield, (Photographic
 Interpretation Unit), 54
Ford, 49
Hunsdon, 58
Leuchars, 59
Manston, 59
Matlask, 59
Medmenham, 50, 53, 57
Royal Australian Air Force:
 Squadrons:
 No.400, 59
 No.453, 48-9
Royal Canadian Air Force:
 Squadron:
 No.418, 58
Royal Flying Corps
 Experimental Works, 16
Royal New Zealand Air Force:
 Squadron:
 No.486, 59
Royal Observer Corps, 61, 85-6,
 94, 102, 108-11, 113, 159
Rye (Sussex), 56

St Lawrence, 56
Salvation Army, 95
Sandys, The Right Honourable
 Duncan, 42-3, 54, 115, 145
Schmidt, Paul, 19, 24-5
Shoreham, 81
Skorzeny, SS-Hauptsturmführer
 Otto, 133
Sopwith Aircraft Company, 17
Southampton, 56, 81
Southbourne, 56
Spitfire fighter, 49, 59, 102, 104
Steventon, Flight Lieutenant, 52
Surrey Docks, 63
Sutton (Surrey), 105
Swinemünde, 42
Swingate, 56